Tammy;

I SAW AN ANGEL TODAY

AN EARTH ANGEL'S DISCOVERY

Gratitude and
Love changed my
life and created
these stories-
I hope you
enjoy them!
Marcy

MARCELLINE MOORE

BALBOA.
PRESS
A DIVISION OF HAY HOUSE

Balboa Press books may be ordered through booksellers or by contacting:

Balboa Press
A Division of Hay House
1663 Liberty Drive
Bloomington, IN 47403
www.balboapress.com
1 (877) 407-4847

Because of the dynamic nature of the Internet, any web addresses or links contained in this book may have changed since publication and may no longer be valid. The views expressed in this work are solely those of the author and do not necessarily reflect the views of the publisher, and the publisher hereby disclaims any responsibility for them.

The author of this book does not dispense medical advice or prescribe the use of any technique as a form of treatment for physical, emotional, or medical problems without the advice of a physician, either directly or indirectly. The intent of the author is only to offer information of a general nature to help you in your quest for emotional and spiritual well-being. In the event you use any of the information in this book for yourself, which is your constitutional right, the author and the publisher assume no responsibility for your actions.

Any people depicted in stock imagery provided by Getty Images are models, and such images are being used for illustrative purposes only.
Certain stock imagery © Getty Images.

Print information available on the last page.

ISBN: 978-1-5043-9897-8 (sc)
ISBN: 978-1-5043-9898-5 (hc)
ISBN: 978-1-5043-9920-3 (e)

Library of Congress Control Number: 2018902482

Balboa Press rev. date: 03/08/2018

Foreword

I met her on a beautiful summers night in a desert town that I once
lived in. We were both there to honor people who had passed or were
battling cancer, and to raise funds for research and awareness.
She came up to my table and handed me a song she had written,
and I think that kind gesture was the first step of this journey.
I contacted her about a year later and asked if I could
perform her song at a local singing contest.
She was excited and honored and easily gave her full support.
My brother helped me recreate her song to perform it, and that
recording has affected countless people throughout my life.
While putting the final touches on this dream of mine, I
received constant signs telling me to find this Angel again and
ask to use her song once more to share with my readers.
It was so easy to find her, and the light of her heart shone
through as she whole heartedly accepted my request.
I have spent countless hours trying to figure out how to
express what *I Saw an Angel Today* is all about.
I truly believe it is best explained through the lyrics of this song.
"Angels Together" was placed into my hands and never left my heart.
I am honored and so unbelievably Grateful to offer it to everyone reading,
I Saw an Angel Today.

Angels Together

We're here today, there is no doubt in my mind.
Here for higher purpose.
To spread our wings,
God is asking us to fly,
And always be there for each other.
We walk this path it's been a journey.
Learn to walk, then run now fly.
To soar above with the eagles.
Angels together, you and I.
The time has come, there is no doubt in my mind.
We are here for special reasons.
To lead the way,
guiding others on their path,
while holding hands with one another.
We walk this path it's been a journey.
Learn to walk, then run now fly.
To soar above with the eagles.
Angels together, you and I.
God lights the way, there is no doubt in my mind,
even in our darkest hours.
Let's shine our light.
Make a difference for mankind,
we can do it all together.
We walk this path, it's been a journey.
Learn to walk then run now fly.
To soar above with the eagles.
Angels together, you and I.

Dedicated to Lesley. Thank-you for being my biggest fan and my greatest support. My best friend, my soul mate, and the Love of my life. I am so Grateful to have you on this journey with me. You are the first Angel I see every day, and the last one I see at night.

Love letter to my readers

I Saw an Angel today was written with Love and Gratitude for all the Earth Angels of our World. As these four words are so very important to me, you will always find them capitalized in these stories.

Anonymous Angels

I Saw an Angel Today

She was caring for a young man in a wheelchair.
She was sitting at the back of the building, and I was trying
to hear what she was saying as I did the gardening.
He seemed to have her undivided attention.
She was giving him fluids through a tube in his stomach.
He was handicapped, and she treated him like every other child
on the planet, while talking and laughing as she worked.
She gave him respect, dignity, love, and comfort.
After she finished giving him fluids, she got on a cell phone and
started to video chat with someone for the young man.
He then appeared to be very happy, though it didn't look
like he could physically show much emotion.
She talked joyfully to him after the call.
Laughing and smiling, she cared for him with obvious Love.
Was that his mother? Grandmother? Caregiver?
I wondered how she did it all.
I wondered how she learned to do all these things for him.
I wondered how he ended up in that chair.
I wondered if he was aware of her Love.
I smiled at all the questions flying through my mind.
I smiled at the thought of all the amazing Earth Angels like her.
Maybe to her, this young man was her Earth Angel.
I still wonder.
I wonder if he knows he has his own special Angel.
I do.
I will never forget her.

I Saw an Angel Today

I call him my shopping-cart Angel, and I look forward
to seeing him every time I go grocery shopping.
He never seemed to be around when I got there, but like magic he
would appear just as I finished loading my purchases into the car.
He always approached softly and slowly and would say,
"Good day, may I return your buggy to help out a homeless
fellow?" And then he would smile a shy, little smile.
At first, I thought he was just another bum.
One who was trying to get money out of every shopper for
alcohol or drugs. But maybe he just needed a warm meal.
I always thought he should go get a job and quit begging.
Too many times I just explained that I had one of those
fake coins for the buggies, and it's not "real money."
He would kindly thank me and disappear.
Today, I put on my Gratitude glasses and dug into
my pockets for any loose change I had.
I said, "It's not much, but it's all I have on me."
He smiled as big as the sun and thanked me like
I just handed him hundreds of dollars.
He walked away with a dance in his step and I smiled.
That little bit of change that I would have simply thrown
into the jar on my dresser, just made that fellow dance.
My heart started to sing.
I drove away, thinking of all the times I have judged people
like him in our huge city, and had those negative, low-
energy thoughts about who "I" think they should be.
This one little random act of kindness made me feel so
good, so blessed, so abundant, so happy and light.
I will now carry coins in my pocket every time I go
shopping and I will look for my Buggy Angel.
I will never forget him.

I Saw an Angel Today

She was balancing six children on a double-wide stroller.
Four of them on that massive cart, and two holding the sides.
She was doing her best to answer all their questions, attend
to their needs, and maneuver that large apparatus.
Was she their mother? Their caregiver? Their nanny?
She stopped suddenly.
She magically braced this large load with her legs, and started opening a
door to a coffee shop for an elderly lady with a walker, trying to go in.
She never skipped a beat, never seemed to give a thought as
to how she would accomplish this acrobatic trick.
She just seemed to wave her invisible wings and helped
where she could, with a huge smile on her face.
She held the door and waited patiently for the lady to walk in.
I noticed that all the children went quiet.
The older lady with the walker smiled and thanked
the young lady. She smiled even wider.
Did the older lady see and understand what just happened?
Did the children learn anything while watching
their caregiver give from her heart?
Did anyone else get to appreciate this magical moment?
Will she give another thought to what just made *my* day?
I tried to jump in and assist, but I only seemed to make
things more difficult, so I just backed away and smiled.
The two ladies smiled back.
I will never forget them.

I Saw an Angel Today

He was standing in the middle of a concrete island on a
large, busy city street in heavy rush-hour traffic.
It was pouring rain outside and I was at a stop light in my warm,
comfortable car, trying to get home from a long day at work.
I watched him and wondered why he chose this life, and
why he didn't just stay home on a day like today.
I was thinking he might not even have a home, as our city seems
to attract a lot of homeless people due to the mild climate.
I watched as people gave him change, water bottles, and fruit.
He put his treasures into his large oversized coat.
He turned toward me and raised a large cardboard sign.
I read, "Homeless. Hungry. No spare change too small."
"God Bless."
I have seen similar signs and similar people in that area, but
he smiled. Wow! What an amazing smile he had.
Normally I try to avoid eye contact, but he had the
biggest, warmest, child-like smile I had ever seen.
He seemed very happy.
His smile seemed to open up the clouds, and the
rain appeared to stop. But did it?
I looked around. Nope, it was still pouring.
I smiled back.
That was all I had to give him today, just a smile.
He waved and made a motion like tipping his hat,
and smiled back at me, then took a bow.
The light turned green, and I slowly drove past him still smiling.
I felt warmer in my body and in my heart.
I will never forget him.

I Saw an Angel Today

There were two of them walking across the street as I
was sitting in my car, waiting at a red light.
They didn't look like Angels.
They were dressed only in black and were wearing crazy clothes,
like a mixture of Halloween costumes at a punk rock concert.
They were covered in tattoos and piercings.
Their makeup was dark and black and scary.
They had on backpacks and looked like they were going
home from school. It was about that time of the day.
I was wondering why their parents let them dress like that.
Why they let them out of the house looking the way they did.
I started getting mad at myself for judging these girls and tried to
pivot my thinking, a trick I am learning to see things clearer.
I continued watching them when suddenly they
both stopped right in front of my car.
Without even looking at each other, they turned back.
What happened? Did they forget something?
They quickly walked back, and then they each took an arm of
an older lady with a cane, trying to cross the intersection.
One of the girls held up her hand to me and the
other two lanes of traffic beside me.
Our light went green.
All the cars stayed still and watched these two young girls with
massive Angel wings, help this little old lady cross the street.
I smiled.
Was that due to my pivot?
Was that a message from the Universe?
It was definitely confirmation for me.
I smiled at them.
The one girl holding back the traffic smiled back.
I will never forget them.

I Saw an Angel Today

I heard him first.
Heard him yelling and screaming and throwing things around.
Not an unusual sound from the back alley of our city apartment.
I was trying to ignore the noise.
I turned up the radio and tried to drown out his antics.
I couldn't concentrate on my writing as he seemed to
be getting louder, cursing, and banging things.
It sounded like he was digging in our dumpster.
It sounded like he was throwing everything out onto the road.
I heard breaking glass, and I started getting
concerned for my neighbor's tires.
I was thinking I should call the apartment
manager or maybe even the police.
I decided not to jump to conclusions, and I went to the window.
All I could see over the bushes was paper, tin cans and
milk containers flying out of the dumpster.
He was still yelling and cursing up a storm.
I was thinking he had a mental illness and needed some help.
I was sure I was going to have to go out and help clean up.
I was about to pick up my phone when I saw him jump out.
I opened the window to yell at him to clean up his mess.
That was when I heard him more clearly. He was yelling
about laziness and rich people. I just listened.
I watched in awe as he cleaned up his mess and picked
up everything he threw out. Then he put everything in
the proper recycling boxes beside our dumpster.
He was very unhappy with us.
Our Recycling Angel.
I will never forget him.

I Saw an Angel Today

He was at the front of a classroom full of misfit teenagers.
He looked like he was in his late sixties and had a very long and hard life.
Skinny and dirty, but he tried to clean up for this day. His special day.
He was with a police officer and another lady.
Maybe his social worker? Maybe an outreach worker?
He was talking to the students about his life before he became
an alcoholic, and then how he became homeless.
How talked about how he had a wife, a beautiful home, and a
life mapped out before him, like every "normal" person.
He talked about how alcohol led to the break up of his
marriage and how his life fell apart after that.
He eventually started drinking more at work and that led to a
work accident that stopped him from doing the job he loved.
He went across Canada to try to get away from the memories.
He tried to do odd jobs to make a living but ended up homeless,
because he didn't want to be in the welfare system.
He didn't want to take money from the Canadian people.
He talked about people's prejudices with the homeless.
He talked about his street family with Love and respect.
He explained how he met the two ladies with
him and how they changed his life.
How they got him housing and the help he needed.
He called these ladies his Guardian Angels, yet I think he
was probably a guardian Angel to some of these kids.
I hope they remember these three Angels and their stories.
I know I will. I was Grateful for their time today.
I am Grateful that my teenager and I got to hear these
stories from one of the people in that classroom.
I will never forget them.

I Saw an Angel Today

I noticed she was very pregnant, as I watched her walking down the street.
She was holding her big belly and seemed to be talking to the
baby that would be born any day, any hour, any minute.
The early autumn morning sun seemed to be warming
her face as she looked towards it and smiled.
She was still rubbing her belly gently and seemed
lost in her own world of Love and light.
I wondered about her days to come.
I wondered if she has had children before and
knows how difficult a job it can be.
I hoped she will not be in labour for two days
like I was with both of my children.
I often think that if I hadn't loved being pregnant so much
that my child births would have been much easier.
I started to think about all her days to come and if she
would still be as happy as she was in that moment.
She helped me to remember the good times.
The first feel of the tiny hands, feet, and body in my arms.
The moments of joy at the first smiles, hiccups,
giggles, and tears. First words to first steps.
The moments of unconditional love and trust from
this tiny being, that totally depends on her.
I quickly looked back on both of my sons lives, and all
the joy they have brought to my own life.
I had a tear in my eye and a smile on my face as I watched this young
lady enjoy her quiet morning with her new baby in her big belly.
I gave thanks to the Universe for that moment of reflection
and picked up my cell phone to call my youngest.
I will never forget her.

I Saw an Angel Today

He was walking down the street opening an envelope.
It looked like it was a greeting card. Maybe a birthday card?
He was dressed like he was on his way to a job interview.
He was walking with pride and confidence.
He was very focussed on that treasure in his hands,
like a child on Christmas morning.
As he started to read the card his face began to brighten.
He was smiling, laughing and very happy.
People were kindly moving aside because he didn't
seem to be watching where he was going.
They were getting caught up in his happiness and smiling
back as they passed him. He was unaware.
It appeared he wasn't the only person that card affected today.
Other people's moods seemed to change as he passed them.
My mood changed as I watched him.
I wondered if it was a card from a family member who was
sending loving thoughts to boost his confidence today.
Maybe it was a card from a loved one very far away.
Was it a funny card or just a good luck and best wishes card?
Did they write something personal and funny to
make him laugh aloud as he read it?
I started to think about how sad it is that due to the electronic age
we live in, we don't seem to send cards to people any more.
I cannot remember the last time I sent a card.
I wondered how many more people this Angel passed
today, had the same thoughts as I did.
I wondered if they were as determined as I was to go buy a card
and send it out to brighten someone's day, just as this little
card had. I turned into the drug store to do just that.
I will never forget him.

I Saw an Angel Today

I was scurrying home as fast as legally possible, as I had to pick
up my partner and get to an appointment across our big city.
I managed to leave work early, to make it to the
appointment with plenty of time to spare.
I am always nervous about running out of time and being late.
I turned right off our busy main street and then came to one of the
new round-abouts that are popping up every where in the city.
Having never lived in Europe, I am never sure how to
approach these things or what the rules are.
I saw there was no traffic and started my right turn to go left.
I had a pedestrian approaching the intersection.
He had red hair and a red beard, and he looked like a hiker.
I got really confused, as I have never had a pedestrian
in the maneuvering equation before.
I was taught that pedestrians always have the right of way.
I stopped in the middle of the road to wait to see what he would
do. He didn't seem to see me or care that I was stuck.
He started raising his arms like he wanted to fly.
He started swirling around in circles and seemed to
be going into a dance. A ballet sort of dance.
I smiled.
Still stuck in my move, I just sat and watched him.
He seemed to be telling me to slow down and appreciate life.
"Don't forget to dance and Love the life you live."
He finally saw me and stopped dancing.
He smiled widely and made a motion like tipping his hat.
I smiled back.
He stopped and waved me through the circle.
I was no longer hurried or worried about time.
I will never forget him.

I Saw an Angel Today

She stopped to ask me about the beautiful park we were
walking in. A place I have never walked before.
She seemed as Grateful as I was to be enjoying the day,
and the scenery of this walkway on the lake.
I told her I was new to the area and knew very little, and that I had
just come from the Information Centre that led me to that spot.
She talked about the mountains and the lake.
She talked about feeling like she has finally found home.
She seemed very relaxed and happy.
She was smiling from ear to ear, and her eyes were sparkling.
She seemed to be reflecting my mood completely.
Sometimes I wonder if people come into our lives at moments
like these to remind us of how blessed we are.
Sometimes I think they are heaven sent.
Often, I wonder if any one else can see them.
I have heard many stories of interactions like these
that make people wonder why they happen.
She headed off in the direction I was coming from after I
tell her what was there and how beautiful it was.
I felt the sun on my face, and although it was very
cold today, I was warm and happy inside.
She touched that Gratitude place in my heart.
She asked questions that made me realize how very lucky
I am to be able to call this valley my new home.
She will never know how she lifted my spirits.
Right after our interaction it started to drizzle, and
the most amazing rainbow appeared.
I smiled as big as that bridge the rainbow was falling over.
It is simple things like this day that make special memories.
I will never forget her.

I Saw an Angel Today

This lady seemed very distraught, but patient.
I was trying to help her to reprint some old pictures.
She was worried that we couldn't get the pictures to print.
I couldn't seem to get the equipment to work properly.
That gave us a little time to talk.
She was telling me a story.
A story about a little four-year-old girl that was abducted
by her birth mother and taken away from her father.
The family never stopped looking. Those pictures were for her.
To show her how much she was loved and missed.
The lady I was helping is her grandmother.
She told me about the scenes in the eight pictures.
The only pictures they had left of her granddaughter.
She said that her and her husband were travelling last year and
for some reason had stopped in a mall. They were looking at
pictures of some needed recipients of Christmas hampers.
She recognized one of the faces.
Twelve years later and they were looking at a picture
of their grown missing granddaughter.
It took almost a whole year to find out if it was her in that picture,
where she was now, and if she wanted to re-connect with her family.
The pictures were finally printing as her eyes filled with
tears and she told me she had to have these today.
It just so happened that her granddaughter will be at
the airport tomorrow for a two-hour layover.
Her son is flying in as well, to finally see his daughter again.
I will never forget her story.

I Saw an Angel Today

I look forward to her daily posts on social media.
We have a shared connection and love of horses.
She has created this page to share this love and bond with
these majestic animals and like-minded people.
With these pictures, she also creates beautiful inspirational
messages of hope, love and encouragement for people who
may be needing an uplifting message for the day.
Today, I found a very different message from her.
It seemed she was being attacked for using messages
filled with her faith and Love of Jesus and God.
She posted no apology for her beliefs but a gentle message
that if her God offends you, simply unfollow her page.
She could have added that with over one million followers, the
opinions of a few were nothing to be concerned about.
Instead, she took the higher road of Love and wished them well.
I was inspired and looked up more information on this Angel.
I was curious as to how she came up with the name of her page.
Mafiusu can be translated to mean swagger or boldness. Or, in
reference to a woman, *Mafiusa* means beautiful or attractive.
Very fitting when you look at her messages and pictures.
I am amazed by her talents and her strength.
She is a wonderful reminder to people to be yourself, follow
your heart, and feel free to share your God given talents.
She inspires me to write and to honor my own belief system.
I hope she knows how many lives she touches every day.
You might only need a pretty picture of a horse to uplift your
day, as I do. Or maybe you need a reminder to keep the faith,
be kind to others, forgive often, and remember God's love.
Either way, her *Charity* and kind giving heart, is something
I will never forget.

I Saw an Angel Today

It was the third time I had seen them in that very busy place.
They are a reminder for me that when you open your heart and
your eyes, you continue to see Earth Angels every-where.
I never go to that extremely large mall in our beautiful coastal
city, but it had become a convenient central meeting place for
my son and I. As I waited, I noticed a familiar face.
This Angel always arrives early and by magic or timing,
or other wonderful universal forces, his table and chairs
is always available. I wondered if he noticed that.
He sat down, opened his backpack, and set up a board game.
Almost by cue, the teenage-looking girl with Down Syndrome
arrived and sat down with him to play the game.
I wondered how this came to be.
How this arrangement started, and how they knew each other?
Are they related or was he a social worker of some kind?
Was that a daily activity or a weekly one?
Did he get paid or did he volunteer out of the kindness of his
heart? They really seemed to enjoy each other's company.
How is it that I have seen this interaction so many
times and what was the message for me?
I smiled and watched them playing the game, talking, and
connecting. I thought about how busy my life can be and
that I never seem to have the time to just play a game.
Was that the message for me? Should I simply just meet my son,
like these two, and play a game? Just connect and play?
Wouldn't that be wonderful? I would love to do just that.
My son arrived, and I told him the story as we walked
off and started our errands and our busy day.
We added board games to our mental shopping list.
I will never forget them.

I Saw an Angel Today

My sister and I were talking on the phone about all the Angels
in our lives that have come along to help us, or to remind us
of our connection to each other, on this amazing planet.
We started talking about the ones we remembered from our
childhood, and almost in unison we said, "Mr. Cooper!"
We laughed and shared our memories of that old man.
We think we called him Mr. Cooper from a childhood TV
show, but we were sure that wasn't his real name.
We lived on the Island and as my mother was doing quite
well in her life at that time, she purchased a home for us
in a family condominium in a nice area of town.
We didn't have a lot of memories of that time except for Mr.
Cooper. He seemed to live on the streets, and in our dumpster.
My memory was about shoes, and my sisters was bread soup.
I remember that we had to be careful when we took out the
garbage to make sure Mr. Cooper was not in the dumpster.
One day, just before the start of the new school year, we
all got new school clothes and new school supplies.
Our mother threw away all our old worn-out shoes.
The next morning, they were all back at our door lined up
neatly. My mother was very touched and honored at Mr.
Coopers gift, but she took the shoes to work to throw them
out, so they wouldn't come back to our door again.
That homeless man was so very giving, thoughtful and kind.
He was very aware of his neighbors and tried to help them
out any way he could. He is forever in our hearts.
Over the years, we have had many conversations about
him and his kindness. We often joked about the fact
that he may not have even been homeless.
Maybe he was rich beyond our dreams and just hated waste.
Either way, he was and still is one of those Angels,
we will never forget!

Work Angels

I Saw an Angel Today

She was looking so tired and worn out.
She looked ready to retire.
Everybody loves her so much and miss her even if she's
off for a day. How will they get over her retiring?
She has left a legacy for sure.
She is one of my mentors and I am proud to say, a friend.
She loved to train new people and she was very good at it.
After thirty-four years with the company, she is
absolutely one of our gurus of knowledge.
She tried to handle everybody's questions, concerns, and ideas, while
helping them to grow and become more confident in their own roles.
She seemed to miraculously have time for everybody
and everything, but now it is time for her.
Time to relax and enjoy her days with her husband,
and not worry about her next shift, next task, or the
next project way too large for someone her age.
She is always so happy, polite, and positive about
the day, the people, and the company.
Maybe she has a pair of those Gratitude glasses.
Maybe she invented them.
She definitely showed me how to use them.
There will be a big empty hole where her little body was.
Today was one of the first times in my life I have been sorry to
see someone retire. Not for her. We were all happy for her.
Sad. Sad for all of us who had come to know her, work
with her, learn from her, and had her on our team.
We all wished her the happiest of retirement.
We will never forget her!

I Saw an Angel Today

He greeted us at the gate and explained the history of
the facility, and the programs it offers today.
He took us on a tour through that massive complex
that houses the accused and the guilty.
He appeared wise beyond his years.
Whether dressed in blue or orange, everyone
seemed to like him. To respect him.
He had many stripes on his shoulders that he had obviously
earned, judging by the reactions of the people we passed by.
He answered all our questions about the facility, the
city, and its surrounding communities.
A wealth of knowledge we would likely use for years to come.
After the tour, I waited in the lobby.
Waited for them to call me to that dreaded panel
interview I had failed three times before.
It was almost Christmas Eve and I was thinking that getting this
life long dream job would be the perfect present for my family.
A lady came to get me and took me into an overwhelming
massive office where they were waiting.
Four of them, ready to ask me questions.
But wait. There he was. My tour guide.
Relief. A friendly and kind face to look to in my
struggle for the right answers to give them.
I smiled and relaxed. He smiled back.
His smile was one of the biggest I had ever seen, and
it helped me through that long official process.
I left feeling like I was finally successful.
He called me Christmas Eve to tell me I got the position.
I was finally a Correctional Officer.
I will never forget him.

I Saw an Angel Today

He was talking to another associate. She was crying. She was upset about
something in her personal life. Something about being a single mom.
I know that story all too well.
He was listening. Listening with an open heart as
he always had. Listening with compassion.
He let her talk for quite some time.
Where did he find the time?
He runs a huge retail business and he never seemed to
sit still, but there he was. Still and focused.
Giving one of the two hundred and fifty plus associates
his undivided attention. I recognized the situation.
I remembered each time he had done that for me.
The many times I went to him for guidance, support,
understanding, direction, and just to vent.
I smiled. I smiled at the person he is. I smiled at the
privilege it is to know him and to work for him.
I smiled at the years of working with him.
We started in this company at the same time.
He was a manager in training and I was close
to the bottom of the corporate ladder.
He helped me grow within the company and I now
work beside him as one of his assistants.
I wondered if this lady will be as successful as I was.
I wondered if she knows how lucky she is to have him as her
boss. I wondered if she will remember this moment as I will.
He caught me smiling and starring at them and smiled.
I smiled back. With Gratitude and with appreciation.
I will never forget him.

I Saw an Angel Today

There are two of them.
They are partners in their duties.
One is a police officer and the other is an outreach worker.
They walk the streets of our huge coastal city in the early morning
hours because that is when the homeless are still and sleeping.
They try to find homes for them.
They work hard every-day to get them the medical
and professional services they require.
Often, they simply offer an ear, a drink of juice or coffee, a cigarette,
or a business card for future use, should anybody need anything.
They offer directions to the nearest office where the
homeless can get financial assistance.
They even assist in filling out the necessary forms.
They make connections for them in emergency situations.
They respect our street people and give them the space the
want, if they are not quite ready to talk to them.
They love this part of their work day.
They are making a difference.
They are the silent heroes in our community.
They give me hope for all the homeless people I have seen
in our mild weather city. Too many in this area.
They are amazing at what they do, and everybody appears
to know them, respect them, and Love them.
They are humble and happy to make a difference.
I could spend all day watching them and listening to their stories.
They will always be the Earth Angels on our streets.
I will never forget them.

I Saw an Angel Today

Everyday I walk into that building, I look forward to seeing her
and hope she is working. Hoping to catch her looking my way.
She always makes me feel like a million dollars.
She is always so happy to see me and her face lights up
like the brightest star on top of a Christmas tree.
She will then wave and almost jump up and down with
excitement, like a little girl trying to get Santa's attention.
Today, I was sad and disappointed that she wasn't working.
I went about my day answering a million questions, taking care of
customers and associates. As usual, I barely had time for lunch.
I decided to walk to the food department to find
something to eat. There she was.
She smiled from ear to ear, her voice went up ten octaves,
and she squealed the usual, "Hi, beautiful lady!"
My day was getting tough, but she turned it around instantly.
My whole mood changed. My soul started to shine.
I went over to her trying to match her excitement.
She genuinely and whole-heartedly asked how I was and how
my day was going. I had some-how forgotten the bad stuff.
I started talking about the things I love to do and looked forward to
hearing her wonderful insights, amazingly uplifting advice, and her
constant positive outlook on creating joy in everything we do.
She told me that she loves when I stop by and talk with her.
She told me that she loves talking to me about everything.
I found that really strange, because that is exactly what I
look forward to every-day. Just being around her light.
I always feel like I know her from some-where. Like I have
known her my whole life. Maybe it is her soul I recognize?
I know that smile. I know that heart.
I recognize the energy. I am so Grateful to know her.
I think we all need a daily dose of this Angel.
I will never forget her.

I Saw an Angel Today

He was telling a story at our morning meeting.
We were talking about winning contests.
He was speaking about his parents and about a time that
they entered a contest for a scholarship for him.
He said it was at a tour for a new college and it was
for a four-year tuition. A very big prize.
His parents were thrilled when they got the call that they
had won, but they were quickly disappointed.
Apparently, he was only ten years old and this
prize had to be used within two years.
His parents did not want to see this great gift go to waste.
They put an add in a local paper for a writing contest.
Contestants wrote in about what their dream job
was, and how that tuition could help them.
They received hundreds of responses, they had their work cut out for them.
Reading all the stories was tiring, touching and sad.
Sad that they could not help every one of those writers.
Exciting that they could help one.
They finally decided.
She was a single mom wanting to become a nurse.
Maybe a nurse working with children.
Maybe a nurse working in the emergency room.
Maybe a nurse working in a hospice.
I can only imagine how that young girl felt when she got
the call that she was receiving this grand gift.
I wonder where she is today.
I thanked my co-worker for his amazing story.
I will never forget them.

I Saw an Angel Today

She was smiling ear to ear even though she had
just returned to work after a long holiday.
I couldn't wait to hear her stories.
She loves to travel, and I was excited to hear where she
went this time. What she saw. What she did.
She has been everywhere I can think of to go on our beautiful
planet, and places I have never even heard of.
I am always amazed at her bravery to go on these trips alone.
She has spoken about how she wished she had a travelling
companion, but that not having one would never stop
her from going. Never stop her from exploring.
I have no clue how she accomplishes this on her wages.
I assume she must do nothing else but save money.
I know she takes on part time jobs any-where she can.
Today she was speaking about her trip to Paris.
She talked about all the sites, the people, and the culture.
She had some exciting news to share with us.
She has met two ladies that were travelling alone as well.
They both love to travel and can never find any-one who
can afford to go, or wants to go, without their spouse.
The three of them had a great time together.
They have now made future plans.
Plans of meeting in all of these amazing destinations
and having someone waiting for them.
Waiting to explore and take in the sites.
Complete strangers coming together to fulfill
each other's dreams of travelling.
Next stop Australia, where one of these lady's lives.
I will never forget her.

I Saw an Angel Today

She has been missing from work for quite some time.
She has been going through a few things this year
that has been affecting her health negatively.
She has not really spoken to any-one about these issues
which has led to a vast amount of judgement.
She is teaching me that ignorance causes judgement.
She is teaching me that people judge more harshly
when some-one's actions directly affect them.
She is teaching me how one person's constant absence
from a team can negatively impact the team.
More than all that, she is teaching me to step up and
offer a friendly voice or lend an ear, or simply
a cup of coffee. Something a friend would do.
I am learning that although people go through the same things
in life, they most definitely handle things differently.
As I read her story and see her picture on social media, I
started to cry. My heart and throat started to ache.
Not for the challenges she is facing, but for the way I have judged
her. Knowing that I have absolutely no right to judge.
I am more affected by her story as I have been going
through much of the same issues as she is this year.
I become more aware that because of our similar stories,
I should be more supportive. Less judgemental.
I start to feel very Grateful.
Grateful for the knowledge and the acceptance.
She is now my Judgement Angel.
She has taught me more than she will ever know.
I will never forget her.

I Saw an Angel Today

I am new to the area and the work place.
She doesn't know me at all but welcomes me whole heartedly
by her actions and not necessarily with words.
She has spoiled me with all kinds of baked goodies through
the holidays and recipes we will use together, next year.
She offers all the experience and knowledge of being
a longer resident to our new home town.
She is trying to teach me the ways of this new work
place, but she does this so gently and kindly.
I am between homes and everything I own is
eight hours away with my family.
She offers up everything she can to help me get by.
To help me live comfortably for the next two months.
She respects my privacy and only reaches out when
she appears to sense I need something.
Tonight, I am lonely and missing my family when she
sends me a message to see how I am doing.
I welcome the distraction and the small amount of
human interaction. I wish she could talk longer.
I offer for her to come over and see the new home
she has helped me live in quite comfortably.
She replies that she will see how I am feeling tomorrow.
She finishes the conversation with, "Enjoy creative time."
I think I mentioned to her only once that I love to write.
I am touched that she remembered.
I also take this as a sign to get busy.
She is the first person I think of as I write…
I Saw an Angel Today

I Saw an Angel Today

He was my right hand at work for a long time.
I looked forward to seeing him every morning.
I have watched as he went through the falling in love
process with the girl he now loves and lives with.
I look forward to the day that I receive a wedding invitation
in the mail. I bug them all the time about it.
He kind of feels like one of my own children as I watch
him grow and become an amazing man.
He seems so sweet and giving and kind.
I was sad to hear that he was leaving our company to
go try something new and maybe make a career.
I get very happy when he hugs me every time they stop in.
I still miss his smiles, his warmth and the caring way
he listened to my stories and shared his own.
He made my work days go by much quicker.
He made me feel secure and supported in my position.
His experience and work ethics are hard to replace.
It is hard to find these values in someone so young.
I look forward to seeing where his life leads him.
I am sure he will do well and be successful in anything he
puts his mind to. He is a determined young man.
He reminds me of so many others I have had the privilege of hiring, training,
supervising, and ultimately watching them spread their wings and fly away.
I hope he will keep in touch.
I wished him well today as he came in to say hello, tomorrow
as he says see you later, and each and every day there after.
I smiled as I watched him walk away. Holding his Love's hand.
I will never forget him.

I Saw an Angel Today

She has become more than my mentor, she has become one of
my closest friends. I miss her now that she is so far away.
I think back to the day I met her.
She looked awkward in her high heels.
I sensed she was more comfortable in steel toe boots.
She was interviewing me for a position on her team.
She asked me to wait and walked away.
She came back and told me that she had to be honest and that she could
not offer to pay me what I was used to receiving. She added that the time
it takes me to travel, and the wear and tear on my vehicle, would be greatly
diminished. She also stated that given my experience, she could strongly
predict a management position within two years at this new company.
I was one month shy of the two-year mark when I was
promoted. She smiles so proudly when I tell this story.
She still mentors me in so many ways.
Professionally, mentally, personally, and spiritually.
She is wise beyond her years.
I think I am old enough to be her mother, yet in some
ways she will always feel like one of mine.
She comes across as a strong force to be reckoned with in most
areas of her life, but I have come to know a softer side.
A side that can be torn apart and built back up.
She has worn so many hats since the day I met her.
A leader, a teacher, a friend, a snowboarder, a new driver, a lover
falling in Love, loosing, and falling in Love again. A mother to her
cats, a daughter, a hiker, a food critic, a student, and a mentor.
I love her like a sister.
I will never forget her.

I Saw an Angel Today

I ran into her on the street today.
She was overjoyed to see me and hugged me like a
momma bear, and then smiled from ear to ear.
What a beautiful, joyful smile.
She makes you smile till it hurts, looking at that smile of hers.
She was so very interested in what I am doing, where I am
going and that I am as happy as she seems to be.
She was one of my right hands and I loved teaching
her everything I knew. We were a great team.
Her work ethics are amazing for a girl her age.
She worked circles around most men I have worked with.
Even though she had some health issues, she seemed to
come to work every day out of respect for me.
All the years we worked together, I tried to convince her to
take advantage of her lost benefits and go back to school.
I always thought she could become an amazing teacher.
I could see her in small classrooms teaching children.
Children with special needs or in special circumstances.
I could also see her doing more volunteer work with that heart of
hers. Time to give, that she couldn't afford to do working with me.
I was almost in tears when she said she finally followed
her mother's and my advice and went back to school.
I was not surprised when she said she is getting her Masters
Degree in education to teach Indigenous Children.
I know that whatever she sets out to do, she will
do an amazing job and be very successful.
I hope she knows how proud I am of her.
She is my lightening *Boult*.
I will never forget her.

I Saw an Angel Today

She has the most generous and giving heart.
It seems she gives every bit of her spare time to the charity
work that our work place does for the community.
She is always planning, informing, and executing these
events with love and grace. Giving from her heart.
She has also been one of my mentors for almost ten years, as
she knows so much about the operations of our company.
She is now trying to master three people's jobs in her now
very empty office. She looks kind of lonely in there.
I try to stop by and just say hello, but she thinks I am
only after her chocolate that we all know she has.
I should tell her it's really because I love her stories
about her family, grandkids, and motorcycles.
About the events she is planning and how much they have
raised. Even about something new she has learned about
work, although she is so multi-talented, I get confused.
She somehow still seems to get overly shy and turns a nice
shade of red. Almost matching her hair, depending on what
her hairdresser daughter has done with it lately.
She is so loved and respected and I hope she knows that.
A lot of us would be lost without her.
We depend on her to help us get through a lot of the daily tasks
or even just to stop by for a little bit of "sweetness."
I am getting to know her on a higher spiritual basis and
I am loving the transition of the relationship.
I am excited to see where she goes with her new talents.
Whenever I drive through the town of *Greenwood*,
I think of her and her smile. Then I smile.
I will never forget her.

I Saw an Angel Today

Her name is actually, Angel. She was my team leader for
many years at one of my first places of employment.
She was the epitome of a strong woman in a male
dominant role. She commanded respect.
I often think about her and wish I could tell her how she changed
my life and made my employment life so much better.
She was one of those people that taught you some of the most important
lessons in life. Like a teacher, a coach, a counsellor, a friend, or even a boss.
I was going through a world of issues at home and overall
in my personal life. I was a single mom with very little
money and a very large chip on my shoulder.
Nothing ever seemed to go well at that time and I
made sure every-one around me knew about it.
I was angry, sad, emotional, and not nice to work with.
This Angel sat me down and gave me one last chance.
She was writing me a last warning when she put down her
pen and had a heart to heart conversation with me.
She said, "The easiest way to make your work life better
was to leave all your personal life at home."
Then she said, "We often spend most of our days at work, so this is a
very good practice and it may actually transform your life." She added
that, "Nobody wants to come to work and hear about how horrible
your life is." Then she finished with, "Some people use work to escape
all that crappy stuff and you should learn by their good practices."
She demanded her team be happy and positive. ALWAYS.
Or just leave her store, it was that simple.
I will never forget her.

I Saw an Angel Today

There were probably over a hundred and fifty of them.
I often tell the story about when I worked in the
Twilight Zone, and I am almost never believed.
This was a large big box store where absolutely
everyone loved everyone else.
It was the largest, happiest, most loving environment that I ever worked in.
I never heard one person speaking badly about any
other person in that very big building.
I worked in many different departments in that store
and I was trained, mentored, guided, and supported in
each and every role. Sometimes, I still am today.
Every coffee break and lunch break were hard to leave
as I can only remember laughing and smiling and
teasing each other like brothers and sisters do.
We were also very big on charity work and the turnouts
for all our charity events was out of this World.
When they found out that I was going through a marital
separation at Christmas, they all got together and made sure
that my ten-year-old son never knew there was an issue,
with the largest hampers and a truck load of gifts.
I was never sorrier to have to leave a place of
employment, but I wanted a bigger career.
After ten years, many of them are still there.
I still miss each and every one of them.
I often wish I could have brought them with me on my journey.
My orange apron is still in my closet.
I recommend this place of employment to anyone looking.
I will never forget any of them!

Historical Angels

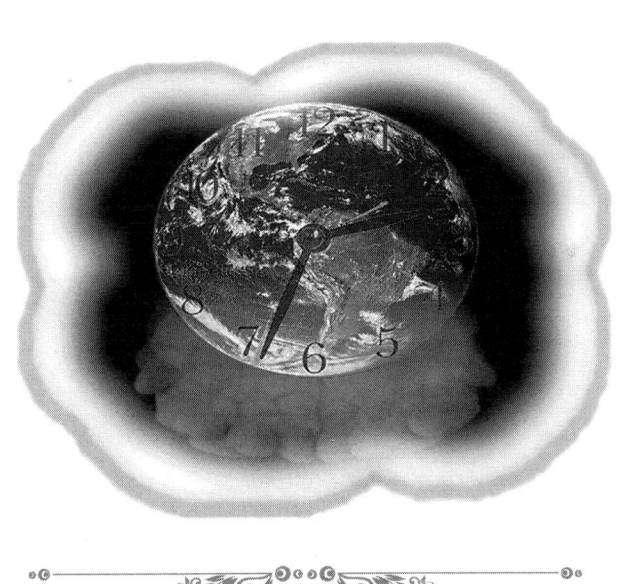

I Saw an Angel Today

Every year at Christmas time, I look forward to seeing
one of his greatest achievements made into a film.
It is a classic film from the World's greatest novelist of the
Victorian era. If that wasn't enough, there was much more
to this Earth Angel than most people are aware of.
He was born to a large family and spent most of
his time indoors reading and writing.
He was sent to work in a factory at the age of twelve,
which probably contributed to his passion of advocating
for children's rights, education and social reform.
As with most writers, his hard life lessons can be
found in most of the characters he created.
I recently discovered much more to this amazing man.
I came across one of his writings that I never knew
existed, and that led me to more research.
His religious beliefs were and are very much the same as mine and I am
more anxious to have that one little book over any others he has created.
He had written this book for his children and
read it to them every Christmas.
It took many years after he passed away, for that book to make it
to print, but I am very Grateful that it was finally published.
He told a story of the meaning of Christmas in simple
language. The World should be reminded of it today.
Especially at Christmas, as I settle in for our usual tradition,
popcorn in hand and waiting for a *Christmas Carol* to begin.
I am Grateful for this Angel from so long ago.
I will never forget him.

I Saw an Angel Today

They are talking about him everywhere as they celebrate a
Federal holiday, in his name, on this third week in January.
This prompts me to investigate more about his story.
I knew he was a minister and activist for the African American Civil Rights
Movement and that he helped change the lives of millions, and still does.
His method was of peaceful non-violent demonstrations,
for which he won the Nobel Peace Prize.
He was responsible for and aided in such historical
events as the Montgomery Bus Boycott, The Albany
Movement, and Selma to Montgomery March.
He was working on the issues around segregated housing, and
the Poor Peoples Campaign when he was assassinated.
After he received his visual wings, he was awarded the Presidential
Medal of Freedom and the Congressional Gold Medal. Hundreds of
streets and even a whole county has been renamed in his honor.
Though his life was cut short by ignorance, his
work and his dream will live on forever.
I feel so much Gratitude for this man's gifts to humanity.
We are blessed that he worked so hard to change the injustices of his
time, and ultimately started the changes the world needed, to grow
into the amazing multicultural society we are becoming today.
We all have dreams.
The Dream he had made one of the greatest speeches of all time and
touched the lives of everyone that day and for decades to follow.
I will never forget him.

I Saw an Angel Today

He is the *Reason for the Season*.
It feels as if the world comes together and celebrates His
birthday. It feels like there is magic in the air.
Every-one appears to be happier. Smiling more. Kinder in
words. Greater in deeds. Hearts full of Love and charity.
Maybe it is in anticipation of being with family and friends.
Maybe it is some well deserved extra days off work.
Maybe it is a time to express to loved ones what is in your
heart. A time to celebrate, to eat, drink and be merry.
He was a teacher, a brother, a son, and a healer.
To some he was a Father, a Rabbi, a King.
Some say he gave his life to save our souls.
I believe there are many messages in his teachings that are
still available to guide and honor the lives of every soul.
However, one chooses to remember the birth, life and death
of this amazing Angel will forever be a choice.
It is hard to deny that something magical happened in history
that brings us together every year at the same time.
It is getting harder and harder to deny that he existed as they
seem to find more proof, every year, that he was here.
I think he made his mark in history and in many hearts.
One only needs to look around at this time of the year, and see his spirit in
the smiles, sparkling eyes and giving hands of most people around them.
The decorated houses, trees, businesses, and people.
You cannot help but smile and feel Grateful.
Grateful for the Love.
Grateful for the life.
I could never forget Him.

I Saw an Angel Today

Very little is known about her and her life.
Many have guessed and many still try to find answers.
I only know that I have always felt a special bond with her.
Maybe because my middle name is the same as hers.
Maybe because I am a mother too and I know firsthand
about a mother's Love and devotion to their children.
I know of the fear and the pain of worry that a mother has.
Maybe because I have often felt her presence.
I have prayed and spoken with her many times.
Often feeling the Love, she sends to me and my children.
She was part of the most historical event of many religions.
Without her, it is hard to say where the World would
be today, and where religion would be today.
Some say she was a Virgin Mother.
Some say she was and is a Saint.
Some say she is the Queen of the Angels.
I call her Mother of all Mothers, Unconditional
Love of All that is and ever will be.
She was so very brave, when she was told that she was to
carry and birth one of the greatest teachers of all time.
She took a chance of loosing her husband to be, and her
own life, in what she believed she was meant to do.
She probably devoted the rest of her days to her
child's life and watched as they killed him.
She then probably carried on his teachings and devotion to
all of mankind, and it feels as if she still does today.
I know that she is still in the hearts of many.
I am so very Grateful for her life, her gift, her devotion.
I will never forget her.

I Saw an Angel Today

I remember standing at his feet at one of the greatest
memorials I have ever or will probably ever see again.
He was a great man and his statue made him look like a giant.
A father to a country.
I was just a child on that trip, but I was impacted by him.
I saw him again about fifteen years later, looking at
his face carved into the side of a mountain.
I have always felt that he was one of the most loved
and one of the bravest leaders of all time.
He was the founder of equal rights, justice, and liberty.
He was a lawyer and politician, two of the most hated
professions, but he was still loved by so many.
He closely supervised war efforts and especially in the
selection of one of the greatest Generals of all time.
He changed the face of his country with his beliefs,
and his passion for the rights of all people.
He gave a speech at a memorial that went down
in the history books and is often quoted.
One only needs to read his speech from that day in Gettysburg,
to understand who he was and what he believed in.
The way we all should believe today.
I was seven or eight when I read his speech.
I remember it impacted me then, and it still does today.
One could say, "Four score and seven years ago," or
"government of the people, by the people, for the people,"
and you would know exactly what they are saying.
I am probably one of the least political people I know, but I
am so very Grateful for him and his time on our planet.
I will never forget him.

I Saw an Angel Today

She was only thirteen when she was visited in her fathers'
garden by Archangel Michael and two other Saints.
She was asked to support her would-be King and help
recover France from English domination.
Three years later she asked a relative to take her to a nearby town where
she would convince a Commander to take her to the French Royal Court.
He laughed her off, so she returned the following spring
and gained the support of two other soldiers.
After a prediction of a military outcome several days before
the messenger arrived, she was granted escort.
She was dressed as a male soldier to help her get
through hostile territory on her journey.
She impressed the soon to be King, and because they had
exhausted all other war efforts, he placed her at the front
lines of the battle with her beloved banner and sword.
As she was only with the battles for a very short time, the
English proclaimed she was possessed, because there was no other
possible way a young peasant girl could defeat the English.
About one year later she was captured and put on trial.
In her **Kangaroo Court Trial**, it appeared she was executed
mostly for cross-dressing. She insisted she remain in military
clothing and short hair, throughout her incarceration, to
make it more difficult to be molested or raped.
She was found guilty and executed by burning.
Until her dying breath, she claimed she was divinely led.
She will be forever remembered as a brave and active woman.
She has since been declared a Martyr and become a Saint.
I will never forget her.

I Saw an Angel Today

I remember my grandfather speaking about this Historical
Angel all the time, when I was growing up.
It is funny that today, I don't recall if it was good or bad.
I believe that because my grandfather was a young man, new husband and
father in England at that time, he was definitely influenced by this Angel.
I have only recently been made aware of the many
facets of this man throughout history.
He was a historian, writer, artist, army officer, military
advisor, British politician, and a Prime Minister, twice.
He led Britain to victory over Nazi Germany during WWII.
He even helped a young lady become a Queen.
It appears his whole life was about service to humanity.
Some say he suffered from depression, and I believe his writing
and painting helped him through his darkest moments.
He suffered a serious stroke at age seventy-nine, while serving his country.
He retired the following year but stayed in Parliament for another ten years.
He earned his wings the year after.
It appears that most of his life was dedicated to leading the people
through some of the most horrible war times of our history.
I am sure he was heaven sent.
I am interested in learning more about his artistic
life as I search for some of his work.
I have found many quotes of his that could offer great
insights, but also a few laughs to help change a mood.
I believe he was an amazing man.
I will never forget him.

I Saw an Angel Today

She was born into a very wealthy family, but she felt she
had been given clear messages from God to serve.
Thank God, she had a father who believed that women
had a right to an education and supported her financially
while she studied the sciences and nursing.
She fought against the beliefs of her time that women
should be married, just stay home, and have children.
She became the Founder of Modern Nursing.
She created the first secular nursing school of the World.
She received messages about the horrific conditions of wounded
soldiers and gathered thirty-eight other volunteer nurses, that
she had trained, and then headed overseas to assist.
When she arrived, she witnessed the horrific conditions
of overworked medical staff, poor hygiene practices,
mass infections and indecent food preparations.
She sent a plea through the media and was given
a new hospital with sanitation controls.
They say she was responsible for reducing the
death rate from 42% to just 2%.
She was also a writer. She wrote about cleanliness and good hygiene
practices and even wrote a simplified book for people with literacy issues.
Her *Notes on Nursing* is probably still used today.
Somehow more than all of this, was her messages of hope and faith. She
walked the halls of the hospitals, checking on the wounded soldiers when
all was so very still and quiet, and became known as The Lady of the Lamp.
Also known as the Ministering Angel.
I will never forget her.

I Saw an Angel Today

I could not figure out why I felt so anxious, sad, and quiet
yesterday. I felt like I was battling time and I was losing.
Then I got the news today.
One of my biggest Earth Angels, mentors, guru's, guides,
teachers, and as quoted today, "The closest thing to a living
saint," received her well-earned wings yesterday.
As I write about her in my Historical Angels chapter, I
know her legacy will go down in the history books.
She was a visionary, and some would consider the
Founder of the Self-Help Movement.
She devoted her life to helping others and teaching others
about the incredible ability of the body to heal itself.
She wrote about the processes of healing your body, mind,
and soul and spoke about her work around the World.
She then began putting her workshops on paper and that
created the most amazing book I have ever read.
The most inspiring part of her story, for me, was that she
self -published her work and the book went viral.
More than fifty million copies sold.
From the phenomenal work she did with support groups of
AIDS patients, to her Legacy Foundation and Publishing
Company, she has changed countless lives.
She continues to touch lives everyday through her books,
cards, videos, and the amazing team she left behind.
It was one of my life dreams to meet her and hug her.
I will have to wait until I get my own wings.
So long my friend.
You have *Healed My Life* in so many ways.
I will never forget you!

I Saw an Angel Today

I cannot believe it has already been twenty years since
we lost our princess. It seems like yesterday.
I can still feel the sorrow of millions.
As we watch her children become the amazing men they
are today, I wish she was here to experience it all.
My family tapes every show about her legacy.
I was astounded to learn even more about her today.
I don't know why I never heard about the work she did
with the homeless. Walking the streets, meeting them,
shaking their hands, and listening to their stories.
This hit close to home for me as I personally know two
Earth Angels that do this type of work, and the difference
they have made to many homeless people's lives.
I was aware of the amount of work our princess did with the children, the
sick, the poor, the people affected by war, and even just stopping to hold
someone's hand or smile that amazing smile. Work we will never forget.
As I watch her boys speak about how playful, free spirited, strong, wise,
and brave she was, I am filled with the same emotions of twenty years ago.
So again, I search, I watch, I read, and I still miss her.
I am still amazed to find all the things that she had
done in her short life in her role as a princess.
She was a gift from God.
A symbol of our unity.
A picture, a voice, and the presence of Love.
She will forever live in the hearts of millions.
England's Rose.
We could never forget you.

I Saw an Angel Today

I came across a cartoon picture of him shedding his pacifism wings, leaning
them against a World Peace directional sign and rolling up his sleeves,
while holding a sword with the word "Preparedness" written on it.
A face that is easily recognizable as his name has
become synonymous with the word "Genius."
Over the years I have tried to understand his work,
but Physics has never really interested me.
This cartoon, however, led me to try to understand
the non-scientific side of this Angel.
He was partially responsible for the research and development of the
nuclear bomb, calling it one of the biggest mistakes of his life. He believed
that the alternative to the Germans creating it first, far outweighed
his beliefs, so he signed a letter alerting the authorities of his fears.
He was also a huge supporter of civil rights and believed racism
is a disease handed down from one generation to the next.
He probably expressed his passion for humanity so openly due to
the fact he had to leave his home country for fear of not being able
to teach, and possibly even of being captured and put to death.
He had a deep love of music and his quote about how
he thinks, daydreams, finds most joy and sees his life in
music, made me smile. A feeling I know well.
I may not understand the *Theory of Relativity* or his *Miracle
Year* of four of the most amazing scientific papers ever
written. But I do understand everything else this Angel has
contributed to in his seventy-six years on our planet.
I will never forget him.

I Saw an Angel Today

She said, "By blood I am Albanian. By citizenship I am Indian.
By faith, I am a Catholic nun. As to my calling, I belong to the
World. As to my heart, I belong entirely to the heart of Jesus."
She knew from a very early age that she wanted to be a
Missionary, and by the age of twelve, she was convinced.
She left home at the age of eighteen to join the Sisters of
Loreto in Ireland, to help her to learn English.
Eight years later she took her solemn vows in India.
She served as a teacher and a headmistress for nearly
twenty years, when her real studies began.
She was sent to learn and serve, by living with the "poorest
of the poor." She replaced her habit with the (now well
known) white cotton sari with the blue trim.
She founded her first school and then began tending to the poor and hungry.
She had to beg for food and supplies while struggling with
doubt, loneliness, and temptation to return to the convent.
She gained a following of young women who would
become the Missionaries of Charity.
She opened her first hospice where those dying could die with dignity.
Muslims were read the Quran, Hindus received water from the Ganges,
and Catholics were given their Last Rites. She said, "A beautiful
death is for people who lived like animals to die like Angels-Loved
and wanted." Thoughts, ideas, and actions ahead of her time.
Six hundred and ten missions, schools, and shelters
in one hundred and twenty-three countries later, she
passes with a legacy and ultimately Sainthood.
I will never forget her.

I Saw an Angel Today

I heard it was International Day of Non-Violence and
thought that had something to do with D-Day.
I was excited and surprised that it was in honor of one of the
most amazing Earth Angels I have ever heard about.
I knew that he was one of the greatest, most inspiring people
of all time as I have seen so many of his quotes.
He appeared to have lived his life in service to others.
He set out to become a lawyer which probably laid the
foundation of where and how he started his work.
After arriving in Africa, he faced discrimination due to his
skin color and heritage. He was not allowed to sit, stand, or
walk in certain areas, or he would be kicked and beaten.
He wrestled with the thought of returning to India
or staying and protesting for human rights.
Thank God, he decided to stay where he was most needed.
He helped the Indian Community of South
Africa become a unified political force.
He returned home and led India to independence.
He has inspired many movements for civil rights
and freedoms around the World.
He was imprisoned many times and for many years.
He was well known for his peaceful political fasts,
but also did long fasts for self purification.
Two of the quotes I love most are, "You must be the change
you wish to see in the World," and "live as if you were to
die tomorrow; learn as if you were to live forever".
He was the first to receive "Honorific Mahatma,"
which is now used Worldwide.
I will never forget him.

I Saw an Angel Today

As I watch one of my current favorite TV shows about a lesbian, bi-racial couple, and their house of multi-cultured foster children, I am inspired with how far we have come in sixty some odd years.
For some reason another Rose pops into my head and
I am anxious to sit and write her story.
Though there were many Angels before her that performed
similar acts, she was the one most remembered.
She remembered that as a young student, she would watch the
school buses filled with white children go by while the black
children were expected to walk. Usually many miles.
She thought these customs were normal, until she married
a man who was a member of the NAACP.
Ten years later she became active in the Civil Rights
Movement and became their Secretary.
After twelve years of being involved in countless cases of
brutal racial injustices, she had reached her limit.
She boarded a bus and sat in the "colored section."
After the bus filled the "whites-only" section, the bus
driver moved the sign and told her to move back. She
refused to give up her seat and she was arrested.
That was the beginning of a massive bus boycott that lasted three
hundred and eighty-one days, and some say the end of segregation.
She worked the rest of her life for equality and human
rights, and she was named the "First Lady of Civil Rights"
and the "Mother of the Freedom Movement."
As I watch my favorite show, I wonder what she would
be thinking if she were sitting beside me.
I will never forget her.

I Saw an Angel Today

There were so many, and I could fill a book with all of them.
They were the writers, composers, artists, inventors,
chemists, biologists, and philosophers of our History.
They were responsible for the ground-breaking way of
everything we consider to be normal today and tomorrow.
Yet we are inspired, quiet, thoughtful, and reflective
when we look at and study their work.
They all had amazing stories and have all
contributed to our culture and interests.
They are loved, respected, honored and admired as
teachers and guides for many of us today.
Some of their work is worth millions and some had
hardly received pennies for their contributions.
I am amazed and wonder how they ever came up with some of the ideas
and inspirations that became their life's work. Their passion, their purpose.
Sometimes I feel like they were divinely driven.
That they were all working with a higher consciousness.
That maybe they had Angels sitting on their shoulders
and inspiring them and guiding them.
I often feel exactly like that when I write.
I can relate to the inspiration, the love, the passion, and
the drive. The excitement of the finished product.
The hope, dreams and desires that come with the thoughts
of how this might help somebody, someday.
As I reflect on ALL of the amazing Angels of our History, I am
filled with the appreciation of them all, and the ones to come.
Including you and I.
I will never forget them!

Family and Friend Angels

I Saw an Angel Today

Actually, I heard an Angel today upon waking from a great sleep.
I had finally heard my mother's voice.
She received her visual Angel wings a little over eight months
ago and I have been looking and listening for signs or messages
from her since. Just to know that she was near.
We always joked about how we would like to hear from "the other
side," but we also didn't want to get scared out of our pants.
This morning was a wonderful way to hear her.
It was simple and light and I hope I got the
message loud and clear. I am sure I did.
She came through the radio in my waking dream and
said, "Marc, Little House on the Prairie is on!"
I have been going through a lot of emotions about moving back home to the
mountains, so that was a profound message for me. One I needed today.
It cannot happen fast enough for me, as I believe the move
could afford me more time to concentrate on my writing.
A few tears escape. Tears of Gratitude.
A warm feeling of knowing she is still here.
A peaceful feeling that I am making the right decision.
An excited feeling of returning to one of the places I love.
I am feeling like I have gone full circle.
Mom always wondered why we love the area so much.
I always thought it was because it was the one place we
were a complete family, living with both parents.
Also most of our fondest, young adult memories are there.
It may not be a "Little House on the Prairie," but
it is the same feeling in our hearts.
Thanks Mom!
I will never forget this message.

I Saw an Angel Today

She was building another dragon.
She was in her glory, working her artistic magic and creating
another piñata for a child, with all of her Love.
For a smile? To see the little faces light up? For Gratitude?
I don't think so. I think she just loves to create.
To express her talent through her hands.
To have an image in her mind and bring it to life.
Then to give it away.
Give it to a child for their party.
A theme, an event, a grand finale.
Do the children see the hours of work and the love poured
into this dragon? Or do they just want what's inside?
They can't wait to hit it. To smash a hole into it
large enough for the candy to fall out.
Then to watch all the treats fall from the dragon and
scoop up their rewards. Candies and small toys.
This will probably make her have so many mixed emotions as she watches
the children having fun, laughing and playing. The dragon looking on.
Then to watch it get destroyed. Watch all her work left
in pieces and discarded like a fleeting thought.
The children will have fun. She will be happy. It will be
marked as one of the best parties they have ever gone to.
There will be pictures at least.
Memories of a massive dragon piñata that magically appeared and
was slain. Not much left but broken pieces of paper mache.
Another one of her creations. Another gift from the heart.
Left to memories and pictures.
They will never forget her or her dragon.

I Saw an Angel Today

He has the bluest eyes when he is happy and in Love. The
broadest smile and a laugh that is infectious to his audience.
He suffers from back pain, migraines, depression,
and too many ailments to understand.
He is strong-willed, loyal, and kind.
He loves to tease and play with everyone, and he has an
amazing sense of humor. Sometimes, a little twisted.
He suffers from a broken heart and appears to want to live
alone now. Maybe a little afraid to get hurt again.
However, his door is always open.
His home welcomes anyone who needs shelter.
His last meal or his last clean shirt is given without thought
or expectation of anything in return. Just like his mother.
He is amazing with his hands and it appears that
he can fix anything he puts his mind too.
He is especially good with vehicles, which keeps him
very busy with friends and family needing help.
Today, he was telling me how excited he is to be a grandfather.
His eyes were sparkling like a kid with a new toy.
He talked about how he will spoil the child rotten, fill him up with
sugar and then send him home. Then he laughed mischievously.
I am so happy he has this new focus in his life.
I know he will be an unbelievable grandfather, as
he was an amazing dad to his two girls.
He seemed to have a spring in his step as he
said good-bye and walked away.
I smiled and thought back to his family, and all our memories.
I am so happy we found each other again.
I will never forget him.

I Saw an Angel Today

I was arriving home very early in the morning after too
many hours at work, and I was completely exhausted.
Upset that I didn't find an Angel today.
There they were. The two of them.
They jumped up into the window because they
recognized the sound of my car.
I could see they were "talking" to each other about mom being
home. Maybe we can play. Maybe we will get some treats.
I could almost hear them purring or "trilling" like they
do, when they get excited and want to speak.
They looked happy that the family was all together again.
They looked like they were smiling as they rubbed their little
faces and bodies all over the windows and screens.
I waved and called to them and then they both went into long
stretches, seemingly telling me to hurry up and park.
I was immediately happy, peaceful, and calm.
The stresses of the day far behind me.
Love, attention, and Gratitude ahead.
I couldn't wait to see them as I parked and gathered my things.
I thought back to only a few months ago when these two
little sisters came home. So tiny, so sweet, and so shy.
They seemed to have tripled in size as the Manx do.
They are so different in their markings and their demeanor,
but they really seem to love and respect each other.
They have brightened our days.
I suddenly realized I have seen my Angels today.
Pet Angels are probably the most forgotten Angels
in a lot of peoples' very busy lives.
I will never forget them.

I Saw an Angel Today

She raised five children practically on her own as the children's
father never supported her emotionally or financially.
She sacrificed a lot of hopes and dreams to take care
of them. To ensure their needs were met.
She did the best she could without a mother
figure to teach, guide, or support her.
She taught her children to be strong and to
stand up for what they believe in.
She taught them never to judge others, and to
always try to help others in need.
She has always been too proud to ask for help.
She worked two and three jobs to take care of her children
and to make sure they had all their basic needs.
She still works hard to help them any way she can, even
though they are all grown with children of their own.
For some minor, seemingly crazy reasons, three of these children
never call her or even send a letter or birthday card.
She thinks that this is an opportunity to finally fulfill her dream of writing.
The one she put on hold for fifty-one years, when she was
invited to move to New York and write for a living.
She kindly and heavy-heartedly declined, as she had
one baby at home and another on the way.
She always said that if she could do it again, she wouldn't have changed
her mind, as the other three children would probably not have been born.
She opens her laptop and begins to write.
I cannot wait to read her stories.
I will never forget her.

I Saw an Angel Today

She has the most beautiful eyes and long white hair.
She has golden brown skin from sun worshipping.
She has the kindest smile and an amazingly soothing voice.
She is wearing a white dress and I think I recognize her.
Yes, I do recognize her.
I have seen her driving around town in a huge blue car.
I have noticed that she always looks so peaceful and
happy. Always smiling at nothing and everything.
She is talking to a lady about being spiritual and that
we all have amazing gifts to use and share.
I invite myself into the conversation as I know the lady
she is talking to and I don't feel like I am intruding.
She smiles in welcoming.
She continues speaking about how the Universe and God
are one of the same, and that everyone's "God" is the same
energy. Just different names given by different religions.
She talks about the countless books she has read and
the many spiritual journeys she has been on.
She talks about Crystal Healing and Reiki and
how everyone has a sixth sense.
A Knowing. A "Mothers Intuition."
She looks at me and smiles.
She seems to look right into my soul and hug me with
those beautiful almost purple looking eyes.
She talks about soul agreements and about how we have chosen our
family and friends, long before we came to our beautiful blue planet.
I am sure I have just met my own special Angel.
I will never forget her.

I Saw an Angel Today

I recognize this face. These beautiful brown eyes.
It is like holding the same little body almost thirty years
ago. The same little nose, little toes, and little hands.
He is quiet. Sleeping peacefully from a big day.
I am proud.
Proud to be in his life and part of his family.
I am feeling the Love of the Universe, and not
just the love of a proud grandparent.
The love of a proud parent as well.
He is already amazing with him.
So gentle, strong, and proud to show off his son.
Easily adapting to the new roll of being a father.
He is letting his wife rest and taking care of his newborn.
He is changing him and doing everything like a skilled
parent of three or four, but this is his first.
Could it be because he and his brother are so far apart in age
and he learned how to do these things fifteen years ago?
Could it be because he has so many little nephews?
Maybe it is just instinct and Love.
I am filled with joy thinking of how lucky this
little guy is to have him as his father.
Thinking of the years ahead and all the new
memories to create. A new larger family.
The biggest epiphany I have, is knowing that all the decisions I
made in the past, came down to this one magical moment.
This perfect moment to let the past be the past.
Let the Love shine through today and growing forward.
I could never forget them.

I Saw an Angel Today

She has four girls and one boy.
She was a single Mom trying to raise five children
on her own. The youngest in preschool.
She seemed to always be coming or going from work.
Her door was always open, day or night.
Teenagers were constantly walking in and out.
If they were around at meal or snack times, they are offered
a plate. She probably had to buy a box of tea a day.
Some how she always had enough.
She sings like an Angel and we would gather to listen.
Sometimes the songs were sad, but usually songs of hope.
Every-one calls her Mom.
She still seems to have time and energy for every person
that comes through her door. Children and adults.
She is so amazing!
Open hearted, down to earth, kind, and loving.
Today, she was helping her daughter do a fund
raiser for an anti-bullying campaign.
I pitched in and helped as much as I could, but she didn't
seem to need me, as she still has endless energy.
We talked about the old days and how things have changed
but have some how, kind of stayed the same.
I am so Grateful that her family is back in my life.
We still have gifts to offer each other.
Gifts of experience, time, energy, and Love.
Her smile and laugh still fills my heart.
I will never forget her.

I Saw an Angel Today

She struggles with extreme pain every day.
She has very limited use of her right arm.
She was hurt in an accident when she was in a deep sleep,
and now she suffers from a neurological disorder.
She is barely able to function normally anymore.
She no longer can do the job she has done for over fifteen
years, helping so many people on the streets.
She struggles with her identity.
She wonders what else there is. What she can do for
the rest of her life. Who she can become after fifty years
and with only fifteen more to retirement.
She has searched and studied as she gathers information.
Something she is very good at.
She has an idea.
It involves supporting, teaching, and creating awareness.
Helping people with the same condition.
Helping their families to understand and support
the person in their life with this disorder.
Maybe make a video, some flyers, or a website.
How does she do that? Think about others and
how they can benefit from her pain?
She opens her laptop and begins to make some notes with her
left hand. Painfully trying to re-learn how to write.
She is smiling with the thoughts of how she can create it.
I am amazed at her ability to change her situation into something
positive. Something that will ultimately help others.
I will never forget her.

I Saw an Angel Today

He flies in and out of my life, always with perfect timing.
He is the big brother I never had.
He has the most contagious laugh and hugs like a big bear.
No matter how much time has passed since I saw
him last, we pick right up where we left off.
Sharing our stories, our new-found knowledge, and love for
the peace and serenity of his home in the mountains.
He has a new story now.
He is living on top of this gorgeous mountain and
has managed to find a way to help people.
He makes weekly shopping lists for his neighbors.
Shopping lists of building supplies.
Knowing him, he will shop for other little things too.
He then takes a whole day of his time, drives into the
bigger city, and shops for his mountain folk.
He buys the items they need, and helps them with their
projects, by simply giving advice and direction.
He loves to talk to them and to offer whatever he can.
Everyone appears to love, respect, and appreciate him.
His amazing carpenter hands and handy-man knowledge is
exactly what these people are needing in their lives at this
moment. Maybe they just need someone to talk to.
I know he thinks he is just trying to make a living,
but his giving heart expresses so much more.
I think he is heaven sent.
I am proud of who he is and that I have the amazing
ability to call him family. To call him my brother.
I cannot wait to see him again.
I will never forget him.

I Saw an Angel Today

It seems she has been there my whole life.
I cannot remember my life before she was in it.
We met in middle school when she was called to the
office and I thought they had called me.
We both arrived at the same time and announced who we
were and then looked at each other in amazement.
We had almost identical names. A friendship was formed.
She and her family have been there throughout my life
sharing, caring, and helping in so many ways.
Her mother helped me raise my oldest when I was a single mom,
and I still cannot believe she got her visual wings so early.
She is missed at every event her daughter hosts, and she
hosts so many. It seems she is always creating a party for
something. She is amazing at making people feel loved.
Today, she is helping me create the party my mother
always wanted for her Celebration of Life.
She has opened her heart and her home for the food
preparation and shared her talents in making the memory of
this day, that honors my mother's life on our planet.
She has helped us create the most amazing Memory Boards
that displays the largest aspects of who my mom was.
My sister and I could not have done this without her.
She was there from sorting through all of mom's things, to
making sure that every person received a small memory of
mom, and then making sure everything was cleaned up.
There were many other Angels on this day that we are so Grateful
for, but this Angel has been there for over thirty-five years.
My oldest and dearest friend. A part of my family.
I will never forget her.

I Saw an Angel Today

He is wise beyond his years and I am so blessed to have him
in my life. He is my dearest friend's beloved partner.
He agreed to be my youngest son's Godfather and appears
to take this title seriously. He still looks at my son with
Love and seems to speak to him with from his heart.
One day I watched him take my seven-year-old for a walk
around their beautiful yard and talk with him.
I smiled with a tear in my eye.
Later, I found out what the talk was about.
He took my little guy to the creek and explained how the
creek flows to the ocean, evaporates to the sky, falls in
the rain, and repeats the process all over again.
He explained that it is much easier in life to go with the flow
than try to go against it. What a lesson for both of us.
I will remind my youngest about this talk on many occasions.
I know my son has been honored to have him in his life.
I have been Grateful for every interaction I have
had with this amazing *Light Worker*.
He has not only taught my child some amazing lessons in life,
he continues to guide my partner and I, at every visit.
Today, we talked about alternative health, and he went out of his way
to make sure we had all the tools necessary to start the process.
He gives from the heart in everything he does.
We are so lucky to call him a friend, and to have the honor
of visiting them both at their beautiful home.
There is never enough time, and we always hate leaving.
A huge Thank-you with all our Love, never seems enough.
I will never forget him.

I Saw an Angel Today

I am so blessed to have her back in my life.
She was gone for about ten years while I went through a horrible
marriage and tried to figure out who I was. But, I thought about
her daily. Missing her every-time I thought about home.
She is the mother of a lost Love, but I am blessed to keep her
in my life and honored she still wants to be in mine.
She has always been one of my "moms."
I sometimes call her my ex-mother in-law, but she is
ultimately one of my oldest and dearest friends.
We have a lot of history in our lives and our paths seem to always come
back together. Picking right up where we left off as if no time has passed.
As I finally move back to the mountains that I have loved since
I was a child, she is still there. She still looks the same.
I cannot believe she will be eighty this year.
I Love hanging out with her and I look forward to the visits.
I Love to cook for her because she appreciates it so much.
She is always willing to help any way she can.
When we arrived last summer, she jumped right in to help
build a camp site. And now, as we build our new home,
there she is giving her time and energy once again.
She loves to dance, and I love to go with her on her outings.
That is when she is smiling the most.
She still has the heart of a warrior, and she still moves
like she is fifty, so it is hard to see her limitations.
She is still searching. Searching for peace of mind.
I hope I can help her find it, as I have a lot of tools now.
I hope she knows I love her like the daughter she never had.
I will never forget her.

I Saw an Angel Today

Our siblings are probably some of the biggest Angels
in our lives, teaching us both good and bad.
I have always believed that we choose our families and
situations in our lives for our own personal growth.
I also believe we have a choice to keep those family
members close or further away for the same reasons.
I remember when we were younger and how close we used
to be, and it is kind of sad we couldn't stay that way.
At the same time, I feel I have learned all I needed to from those
relationships, and I am fine with where we are today.
We all have a life path to follow that brings us family and
friends to help us along the way. To find, to discover, to
Love, to learn, to grow, to Lose, then to find again.
An absolute beautiful process for all relationships.
There are so many situations that each sibling of mine helped
me through, and I am blessed and Grateful for them. Only one
of the four of them wants to grow forward with me.
I have always heard people say that family is the most
important thing in our lives. But, I also believe that family is
the people who have stayed and want to be in your life.
I have a very large family and I feel very blessed.
Many of the people I call family were not raised with me.
My mother came to realize this in her final years.
As her biological family got smaller and her God given
family got larger. Her one and only sibling, estranged.
I am Grateful for the years and lessons with my siblings.
I love them as I let them go to live their own lives.
I will never forget all the good memories, and
I will never forget them.

I Saw an Angel Today

I cannot believe I have finally found her.
Every day I look at her and I try to remember when she
was not in my life. It is almost impossible.
She fills my heart and makes me smile every time I think
of her. My best friend, my Love, and my soul mate.
I found her online while she was going through some very
tough times and thinking she was facing mortality.
Yet she was light-hearted, funny and a joy to speak with.
I couldn't wait to get emails and text messages from
this complete stranger. This new friend.
She loved to travel, and she was so smart, I thought we
could become great friends. Maybe travel companions.
I couldn't wait to meet her in person, but she wanted to wait
until she got back from another tropical vacation.
I sent her emails everyday while she was gone and told her about
what was happening in our great cold Canadian home.
Something to read when she got back.
We finally met and talked to the very early morning hours.
Talked about everything and nothing. An instant
connection. A great new friend. A lasting Love.
My days and years since have been an ever growing, loving,
giving, receiving, non-judgement, accepting and unconditional
love that very few experience, but most desire.
I am so very lucky and so very blessed.
I am Grateful for every day, every month, every
year, and every memory we share.
I cannot imagine life without her.
She is my life, my Love, and my partner for life.
I could never forget her, because she will always be with me.

Health and Wellness Angels

I Saw an Angel Today

There were two people in my young life who had unfortunately
sent me all the wrong messages about health and wellness.
Messages that all the good, healthy food in the fridge
was for their "diets" and we couldn't touch them.
In later years, I came to understand how these messages
would become my greatest enemy, as I now struggle with my
own weight issues, daily, monthly, and even yearly.
I watched them try every diet plan ever published and fail
every one of them. Feeling defeated and discouraged.
The only plan that worked for them was portion
control, exercise and finding joy in their lives.
I can remember one of them would go swimming every night.
It was as if the pounds melted away in that pool.
I think the other one learned much later in life that just
walking every day with a friend helped her.
As I was a long-distance runner I never needed to
worry about food and diet. I just loved to run.
When I got injured and had to stop running, the old
tapes played, and the pounds packed on.
This also began my search for answers concerning issues
in my life that may have caused my weight gains.
The strongest common denominator was fear of food.
Add to that was the processed, quick easy meals for
a busy family, and the lack of movement.
The messages were wrong.
Bless their hearts, they tried.
I have learned from them that diets don't work.
I will never forget them.

I Saw an Angel Today

Some people think she is crazy as she is extremely
passionate about moving and eating low fat foods.
Everything she teaches makes absolute sense to me, which
is why she has become one of my Wellness Angels.
She was an overweight vegetarian with two children when
she decided to *Stop the Insanity* and start moving.
She started just walking around her yard picking up one
baby, walking to the other, switching and repeating.
She also had enough sense to realize that fat makes you fat.
She was amazed to discover how much fat is in processed
foods and hidden in seemingly healthy packaging.
She never claimed to be a physician, dietician,
nutritionist, or fitness and diet expert.
She was just a single mom who figured it out.
Like millions of other women, she had tried every diet
and every fitness plan that was on the market.
She was always amazed that there were not more fatalities in
the gyms she attended, as everyone was so out of breath.
She realized that you need to stay in breath to survive. What a concept.
Move and stay in breath with full resistant movements. Cardio with
breathing. As a long-distance runner, I understood this very well.
I got fit. I got healthy. I ate A LOT.
She was my hero. She is my hero.
Thank God someone figured it out and was brave enough to
bust the system. To bring light to the wellness industry.
Her passion and craziness were uplifting and contagious.
My family thought *I* was crazy.
I will never forget her.

I Saw an Angel Today

These two Angels have changed my life in so many ways
and have introduced me to many more Angels.
They have created a network of Health and Wellness.
They will often offer free viewing of some or all their broadcasts.
A "must see" for every-one.
The most amazing thing about their network is that it's
not controlled by the food, diet, or medical industry.
The cost is minimum when you factor in all the content that it
offers. From menus to documentaries to meditation practices.
There are exercise programs, yoga and Pilates for
many different levels and ailments.
When I think of the amount of money we spend on junk cable
programming, I think this is worth the investment.
They started this channel from the knowledge and strength
they received trying to get his father well again.
They are a strong, healthy, loving and giving couple who could
probably change the world with all the programs they offer. It
is an all-encompassing and amazing viewing program.
They have set the bar for honest, unbiased, and medically documented
information for every person with an internet access.
One would be amazed to discover what is really happening
to the so-called foods that we consume.
The food companies must list the ingredients on the package,
but that doesn't mean we understand them or their origin.
They have taught me that *Food Matters* and that some things
we put in our mouth could actually be very dangerous.
I am so Grateful for their bravery and abilities to
bring this information into our homes.
I will never forget them.

I Saw an Angel Today

He built a resort in honor of his mother who died
from stage four lung cancer and COPD.
The medical industry tried to treat her with an asthma
pump, and never addressed the symptoms.
As she was leaving the planet she told him that he
must build this resort to help others like her.
He then created a unique experiment for four weeks and
changed the lives of the eight-people involved.
Eight people with twenty-two diseases, consuming nothing
but pure fruit and vegetable juices for twenty-eight days.
The documentary of their process was amazing and encouraging.
It had to be worth twenty-eight days of my own life.
Maybe it could have saved my own mother's life.
She passed away one week before trying this program.
Every-thing that I have learned from this Angel has given me
the opportunity to share with others, the possibility of turning
their health around and maybe improving their life.
I have always believed that food was meant to
keep us healthy, and not make us sick.
Preparing fresh live foods was the ultimate lesson learned.
Getting back to the basics.
He has said "If you don't look after your body,
you will have no-where to live."
I have been "Super Juiced," and I continue to incorporate
fresh juices into my life for the nutrients they offer.
He still offers the documentary free for every-one.
He also offers other free programs and I just finished one today.
A "Big January Cleanup" to start the year.
I will never forget him.

I Saw an Angel Today

I am starting to believe that most of the information
about Health and Wellness that I have received over the
years, have come from this one special Angel.
Over the past thirty years, I have watched her share some
of the best diet and exercise information available.
I noticed recently that she seems to be trying some new
regiments but still seems to be using what works.
One can easily search her name with the word "diet" and a
ton of very useful and helpful information pops up.
She, like so many of us, have battled the bulge for far too long.
I have probably tried every "system" she has.
For me it seems that, treating our bodies like a temple and
giving it only "real" food, appears to be the answer.
But it is the hardest solution.
We have created so many wonderful tasting artificial foods
that it is almost impossible to stay loyal to our vessels.
I know that deep down we don't want to abuse our bodies.
I believe there is so much more to weight issues than that.
I think that this wellness Angel has explored and shared,
every possible reason for our weight loss struggles.
I know that an answer for every-one can be found in the thousands
of pages on the internet and hundreds of shows she has done
on the subject. A gift to every one that watches her.
It may not be comforting to her to know that her name
is so associated with that horrible word, "diet."
I hope it brings her joy knowing that she may be the
answer to the biggest struggle someone's life.
I am Grateful she has been one of my *own* Health and Wellness Angels.
I will never forget her.

I Saw an Angel Today

She is married to one of the most amazing leaders of
all time, but she also has her own agenda.
She is passionate about creating a healthier country.
She understands that it needs to start with our future
generation. The children of today and tomorrow.
She has created a Public Health Campaign that aims to reduce
child obesity to just 5% in the next twenty years.
The campaign focuses on healthier food in all schools,
better food labelling, and more physical activities.
She talks about teaching children about gardening, while
also teaching them the science of how things grow.
She speaks about more physical activity and how we all
need to improve our health in just five ways.
Simple small efforts, focusing on a healthier way of life.
She was even involved in creating a music video and a
dance that makes you want to get up and move.
She has posted a cartoon video about what these changes may
look like through the eyes of a child today, and in the future.
When it comes to children and health, this is probably one of the
greatest achievements to ever come out of that big *white house*.
I hope her work will not be forgotten when she gets to move out.
I hope we will all continue to learn from all the efforts
and energy she has created behind this program.
It seems so very simple.
Following this program may be the greatest thing you do
for your children, your family and for yourself.
Look it up and "Let's Move" towards a world without
child obesity. A world of healthy living.
I will never forget her.

I Saw an Angel Today

He was one of my mother's "favorite peeps."
She talked about him almost daily.
I have seen him on many talk shows, including his *own*.
He is a surgeon, an author, and a talk show host.
He continues to bring a wealth of information to his audiences every where.
He has a website that offers past episodes, amazing
recipes and too many other topics to list.
He has been criticized by his peers, government officials, and publications
for being a spokesperson about alternative health and medicine.
I think he is one of those brave Angels that risks his name
and career to bring us all the information we desire.
Topics, products, and processes for us to discern if they work
for us or not. A new gimmick or miracle, we decide.
In my opinion, it's like going through a large store or library.
Either you buy it, or you put it back on the shelf.
He has more knowledge about how things work in the body, as
he is a Doctor, and a lot of people trust him for that reason.
The way he delivers the information and the guests he has on
his shows, help us to make better informed decisions.
I am so Grateful that we have many types of resources today,
to gather information from everywhere and everyone.
I am Grateful that he has taken the time, effort, and energy to
bring us more information about health and wellness.
He has given people many tools to get healthy and happy.
Some may think he comes from the land of OZ.
I am Grateful he is here on Earth for all of us.
I will never forget him.

I Saw an Angel Today

She is a cancer survivor and she is an inspiration.
She is a best-selling author and a wellness activist.
She has a fun and uplifting approach to everything she
brings to the table, her followers, and her "Tribe."
The titles of her books, blogs, documentaries, Love letters, recipes,
and all of the products she offers, speaks to her spirit.
When she was diagnosed, she realized that there was next
to no books or movies about young women dealing with
situations and problems arising out of battling cancer.
She was a dancer, actress, and photographer and she
also studied and majored in English Literature.
I think these talents helped her to create all the amazing
ways that she reaches people around the world.
She is one of my favorite people, and I cannot remember how
I stumbled across her work. I just Love that I did.
I am most attracted to the ten things I have found that she
has written to take any-one to a higher health vibration.
They are listed under her *Tenth Anniversary of Health*.
Her *Decade of Thriving*.
She says that cancer changed her life for the brighter and
better. She now has no evidence of the disease.
Her Oncologist has been noted as saying that there
is no link between sarcoma and diet.
I say the proof is in the juice.
I am so Grateful she has brought so much *Crazy Sexy* information to us all.
I am so Grateful to receive her daily messages
of Love, peace, joy, and knowledge.
I will never forget her.

I Saw an Angel Today

I cannot believe that she worries about weight.
She has always been one of the most beautiful women
I know, and I have always envied her body.
She taught me that everyone has body image issues.
To some people, it can feel like five pounds over their own
perception of "the perfect body," can be just as difficult to deal with
as someone who is a hundred and fifty pounds over weight.
She also believes that weight issues come from fear.
Many different forms of fear.
Maybe one is afraid of having a relationship
or loosing that same relationship.
Maybe one is afraid to speak their feelings, feel their
feelings or even discover their feelings.
Maybe one is afraid of failing at any one thing or
everything. Maybe afraid of loosing something.
Maybe one is afraid that everything or anything they
put in their mouth will cause weight gain.
Where do we get these fears? Where do they come from?
Is it in our genes? Our upbringing? Our social influences?
She has a lot of valid points, ones that cannot be ignored.
I am still trying to figure out where my fears lie, where
they came from, and how they control me.
I still look at her and wonder how she could ever worry
about five pounds. She is so beautiful in my eyes.
I know the beauty of one's soul out shines the outer image.
She has given me a *Krystal* clear view on fear and weight.
She also never fails to tell me how beautiful I am.
I will never forget her.

I Saw an Angel Today

He is one of my favorite chefs.
He is passionate about starting a *Food Revolution*.
He is fighting the school lunch programs and trying to bring
awareness to the value of nutrition for our children.
I have seen programs of him standing out front of
government buildings and filming his battle.
A change for us all. A change for the better.
It appears we have been working so hard at trying to create
a healthier lifestyle for our children, we have forgotten to
pay attention to one of the most basic principles.
What they put in their mouth.
I am guilty of this myself.
Trying to create a career that will afford us some of the finer things in
life but forgetting to carve out time for healthy home cooked meals.
Being so busy with a lot of unnecessary things and plopping
a quick fix cheap meal in front of my youngest.
As my son learns to cook, I try to show him how to make one
meal stretch into four or five, as he heads off to University.
Again, a lot of boxes and cans. Very little vegetables and fruit.
Thank God, he loves apples and demands at least one a day.
Today, as I ran into our local grocery store to pick up apples, I
saw this chef's picture and a sign about healthier food.
He inspired me to take an extra thirty minutes to prepare
something better than my son's favorite frozen pizza.
I am Grateful he is taking a stand against the
fast food industry and child obesity.
I will never forget him.

I Saw an Angel Today

He is a Doctor with his own talk show.
Through his books and programs, he taught me that we
all need to get real about different areas of our lives.
Our health, our relationships, even ourselves.
He can be very scary when you are not ready to deal
with your own demons and your own actions.
He interviews many people with emotional disorders,
addiction disorders, and eating disorders.
Through these shows, I believe he touches many lives.
Some people criticize him, his past, and his opinions.
I think he is another one of those Angels that may not
be for everyone, but he is there for someone.
Someone who may need the information he offers through other people's
stories or even just the resources he offers at the end of his shows.
His wife and son are also involved in offering health
and wellness resources for women and teens.
There are many books and CD's this family has published
that could help almost anyone seeking guidance.
When Life Matters, and a person is serious about
making their *Family come First*, and even *Rescuing their
Relationship*, this is the Angel I recommend.
From *Life Strategies* to *Weight Solutions*, they have
information and workbooks to help any family.
I am Grateful for him, his wife, and his son.
I will never forget him.
I will never forget them.

I Saw an Angel Today

He has one of my favorite fruits in his name, on his
website, his newsletters, and his social media posts.
He also has a last name that sounds the same as one of my
favorite animals that lives in the mountains and forests.
Many people criticize him for his beliefs and accuse him
of misleading people to gain popularity and money.
I have watched and read a lot of his material and I do
not believe that to be his purpose or drive.
He teaches people about being organic and to return
to the way of living hundreds of years ago.
He teaches about growing your own food and living your
best life through raw food and "superfoods."
He is a huge fan of chocolate, but not the kind you buy in a
convenience store. The kind you must search for in its purest
form. He chooses to grow it, study it, and share it.
He has become a gourmet chocolatier, organic
farmer, bee keeper and vanilla grower.
He had a dream, he made notes, and stayed on course by following
his heart and intuitions. He is now living that dream.
I receive daily messages from him of inspiration,
news, and education on many subjects.
Things that resonate with me I take the time with,
and things that don't, I just delete.
A lot of things I share with family and friends.
He is like most people trying to offer what works for them
in their daily attempt at living in joy and Love.
Living your best life.
It is that simple.
I will never forget him.

I Saw an Angel Today

She is probably the highest selling video workout producer
of all time. You can find them every-where.
She is an actress, writer, activist, former model, and fitness
guru. She is an inspiration as she approaches eighty.
She looks as amazing today as she did in the 1980's.
I think she looks even more beautiful today, as she reflects
her beauty within, and shares her knowledge.
She was raised an atheist and is now a Christian with a
feminist twist. She believes God is within all of us.
She practices a meditation where one just sits and breathes
while letting go of all thoughts, ideas, images, and words.
Her newest videos are for women in their *Primetime*
doing yoga for their mind, body, and spirit.
She has been very straight forward and outspoken about many topics
for women like Love, health, sex, fitness, friendship, and spirit.
A Health and Wellness Angel bringing the information
in the form of books, videos, and audio programs.
I am most enjoying her newest adventure as a character
she plays with *Grace*. A woman whose husband has left
her for another man. She re-invents herself with a new
unlikely room-mate, new career, and new passions.
She is teaching women of all ages that it is "It's never too late -
never too late to start over, never too late to be happy."
As I approach my own *Primetime*, I look up to her and
all her lessons lived, learned, mastered, and shared.
She is one of the wonderous women of today.
I will never forget her.

I Saw an Angel Today

I think that it would be biblical beyond measure if the
way to transforming your health and wellness was found
in the Bible. That would be **Beyond Organic**.
He was at the height of his school life and looking
to a bright future when he got very ill.
At the lowest of his medical journey, and when he was about to have
most of his inner digestive system removed, he discovered a better way.
A way that has always been there.
As he was a religious young man, he turned to the
Bible for guidance with food and nutrition.
He started looking for any and all scriptures that offered
lessons about food and healing with food.
He came to learn what I have had a deep inner knowledge
about for a few years. Get back to the basics.
I have always believed that if we got back to the way we grew,
raised, and even butchered our food, the way we did one hundred or
so years ago, we would be healthier and have a healthier planet.
This Angel has taken it so much further and has started growing, raising,
eating, lecturing, and guiding people to eat by the way of the Bible.
Starting like most in the diet world, with a fast.
A fast of raw foods and water.
Mostly vegetables with some fruits.
I think he may be onto something.
There is a belief in my body that he may have been led to
guide and teach many people about food and God.
As always, it is a choice anyone can make.
I will never forget him.

I Saw an Angel Today

I watch everyday as she struggles with pain beyond what
the average human being is capable of understanding.
She has a condition I have never heard of before.
Chronic Regional Pain Syndrome could be the title for so many
people dealing with chronic pain, but it is so much more.
It was easier for me to understand when it was described as the
brain sending signals that the accident is continually happening
over and over again. Like a car door being constantly slammed
on the limb, with burning sensations and a stabbing feeling.
There is a whole different pain scale for this disorder.
Where the birth of a child, cancer treatments and loss of a limb
start and finish one pain scale, this other one starts.
She always sits at an eight to ten on the higher scale.
There doesn't seem to be the right combinations of drugs to
relieve her symptoms. To help her function normally.
So where are the answers?
Is it in narcotics? In organics? In food? In Spirit? In faith?
Is it in a combination of all of these?
At this point, it is an experiment.
Maybe she will be the answer.
Maybe she will be the Health and Wellness Angel sent to offer
relief and answers for all others suffering with pain.
She is so strong and brave.
I cannot imagine how she faces every day.
How she manages to smile and function.
I am anxious to see her journey end.
I am anxious to see if there are more answers to Health
and Wellness in the battle against chronic pain.
I will never forget her!

Spiritual Angels

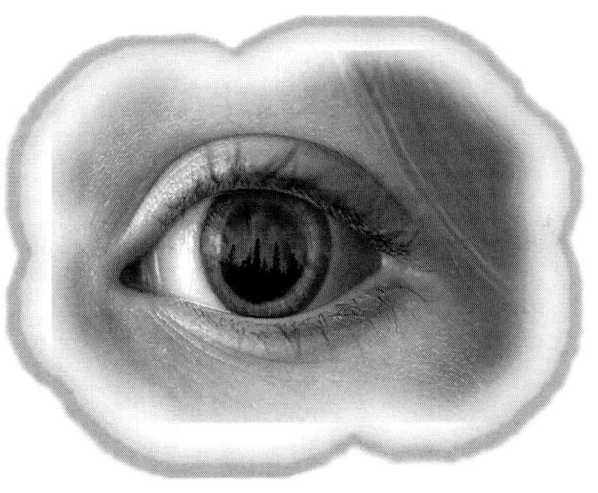

I Saw an Angel Today

I see them everywhere.
They are babies and toddlers on outings with their parents.
Not quite at the speaking stages.
I am always in awe at how they seem to zone in on my energy
and lock eyes with me, seemingly trying to say something.
Do they recognize me?
Do they know the energy of my soul and see it in my eyes?
I try to talk to them in my mind and hope they can hear.
They seem to understand every word I am thinking.
They will get strolled away but they strain to keep watching
me, to keep listening to my mindful messages.
They will often smile at me and their parents will pick up
on my energy game, look at their child, then at me.
They are wondering what is transpiring between their
child and this stranger. They don't seem concerned.
Their parents usually smile and go back to what they were doing.
This is a favorite game of mine while standing in lines.
It is confirmation for me that we are all pure loving
beings of connection in our infant stages.
We are more connected and in Love with everything
and everybody in these young bodies.
If we all could still tune into each others energy of Love,
I always wonder where the World would be today.
I know that when I walk away from these interactions with
the young souls, I am filled with Love and hope.
Hope for a better tomorrow for these little ones.
Trust that they are here to help us learn of a better way.
A better way of communicating.
I will never forget these fun interactions.

I Saw an Angel Today

His book practically fell off the shelf and into my hands,
at a tiny book store I found in California.
The cover was a beautiful scenery of mountains,
a lake, and a man standing on a cliff.
The author claimed he was having a *Conversation with God*.
I immediately wondered how this book made it to
publication and wasn't censored by the church.
I also wondered why God would speak to this *one* man.
What made him so special?
Doesn't God only speak to the highest of the church?
I wondered if I could learn how to do the same.
I spoke to God all the time in my prayers, but could I learn
to hear him? To actually have a conversation?
I opened the book to the first chapter.
I read it in seconds, hanging onto every word and the
next words to follow. I couldn't put it down.
I didn't have a lot of money, but I had to have this book.
I saw there was another book beside it that said it was the
answers to all the questions from book one, two and three.
I figured I could cheat a little and just get that one book as it
was so much cheaper. I felt like I was cheating at school.
I took home the *Answer Book* and soon realized it didn't help me
at all because it constantly referred to the other three books.
It was a few months later before I was finally holding Book One.
I cried through most of that amazing book as it seemed that
this writer was the vessel to all the questions I ever had.
Today, I finished the trilogy.
I am so Grateful for this man, his bravery, and his gift.
I will never forget him.

I Saw an Angel Today

Her book is one of the first books I read in my spiritual journey.
It was recommended to me by my mother who was a
devout Anglican, and knew I was seeking more.
I was working in a prison and looking through the
Inmates library when I came across her book.
As I was becoming more in tune with "following signs,"
I let the Inmates know I was borrowing it.
From the very beginning she talked about looking for our life's
purpose and knowing or feeling like there was something more.
She took a publicity beating for speaking about
reincarnation, meditation, mediumship, and UFO's.
Common conversations today, but not back then.
She quite possibly hurt her career.
I find it funny that even bad publicity is publicity, and
it likely helped her reach more people like me.
I knew that book arrived at a perfect time for me, as it
validated a lot of my own thoughts and feelings.
It definitely started me on my own spiritual path.
It seemed like immediately after reading her book all the Earth Angels
that she wrote about came into my own life in different forms of
books, seminars, gatherings, and even just everyday interactions.
It seemed like only a few days after I opened myself to reading
her book, my own guide, teacher, friend, and mentor arrived.
I am so Grateful for how brave, brazen, and honest that
fiery red headed dancer/actress is in her life.
I am so thankful that she went *Out on a Limb*.
I will never forget her.

I Saw an Angel Today

I am often told how lucky I am to have her in my life.
I couldn't agree more and send countless messages
of Gratitude and Love for her arrival.
She is strikingly beautiful, and I cannot discern if it is
her beauty on the inside or outside that I see.
If we were to dress her up and put wings on her
she would be the epitome of an Angel.
She jokes and calls herself the "Princess of the Universe"
on her birthday. Some would believe this to be true.
She has been the centre of my spiritual journey and has guided
me to a Universe of information on my spiritual path.
She is most definitely one of my guides. My Guru.
She is tuned into all her senses and does spiritual
readings, crystal therapy, and so much more.
She seems to guide every person she speaks to with much
needed information, resources, and knowledge.
She comes from and speaks from the heart. Always.
She honors every person's own path and never seems to judge,
as she has a higher awareness of the bigger picture.
I cry every time I see her as she hugs me with all her Love
and whispers in my ear, "Welcome home beauty."
I believe in soul agreements and I always think back to when
I found her in that tiny little West Coast Island town.
Probably one of the most important things she has taught
me is to stay in Gratitude. Always think of something
to be Grateful for and your life will change.
This lesson, I always try to pass on to others.
Every-one can create the life of their dreams by
the simple daily ritual of being Grateful.
I will never forget her!

I Saw an Angel Today

He is being interviewed by one of my favorite ladies.
He looks very modern and hip for a spiritual teacher.
His face appears to be filled with joy and Love.
I am drawn in by every one of his words and put aside
what I was doing. He has my complete attention.
He speaks of a church that every race and religion attends.
He speaks of a church that is all about Love, joy, and
acceptance. No judgement. No ONE religion.
A trans-denominational community.
He adds that Love is all that there is, God is all
that there is, and Peace is all that there is.
I can feel my mind, body and spirit responding to their
conversation as everything they speak about is what I have
been on the path towards for over twenty-five years.
I am in awe as they talk about *Victim Consciousness*, *Manifest
Consciousness*, *Channel Consciousness*, and *BEING Consciousness*.
I am sad when the interview ends, but excited to
find out more, so I look up his church.
The title is a Greco-Christian term referring to Love.
The highest form of Love.
The Love of God for man and a man for God.
It embraces a universal unconditional Love.
Many of us have had a hard time with the word "God."
I think it was due to our past individual circumstances.
I am learning to see the title as something bigger than
we can imagine. As big as the Universe.
I feel that this man is in tune with Universal Love.
I will never forget him.

I Saw an Angel Today

My personal Guru has always spoken of Ascended Masters and
Arch Angels, so it is no surprise that I am drawn to *The Book*.
One of my bibles.
This author seems to have information on these Gods, Goddesses,
folklore, spiritual, multi-religion beings that feels so very true in my heart.
Information that is hard to ignore. Knowledge beyond this World.
She says that she has been a clairvoyant from a young age.
She says that we all have the same abilities.
I know that when I am doing the work, I feel in tune with the Universe and
that information flows through me that is unexplainable and undeniable.
I feel just as energized and open when I read her books,
work with her oracle cards, and watch her videos.
She has inspired me to follow my heart, write from my
heart, and stay in Love and joy in everything I do.
When I get into my funky moods and cannot seem to tune
into joy, up she pops in an email or on my phone.
As I write this, my phone pings, and there she is.
Telling me about free workshops this coming week.
I am drawn to Angels and they come to me in many forms.
I cannot have a conversation with them like she can, but
I can feel them when I see my Earth Angels.
When I write about the ones who have touched my life.
The ones who have touched many lives.
They call her the Angel Lady.
I call her one of my Gurus.
I will never forget her.

I Saw an Angel Today

In my house, we call him Dr. D.
I have watched him on many TV program fundraising
events and wish that I had the time and money to read
every one of his amazing books. Someday I will.
The titles of his books are like sparks to my soul, and
obviously to many others as he sells millions of copies.
He is a self-help author and motivational speaker.
I recently watched a documentary he filmed about how
you can *Shift* your life into a life of joy, by honoring who
you are and what you love to be and love to do.
If you feel stuck or if life doesn't seem to be bringing you joy
any-more, it is an indicator that you need to *Shift*.
Embrace the things that make your spirit full.
He says that if you want to open the doors in your life than you detach
from the outcomes. You show respect for life. Be sincere and honest, be
gentle and kind, and always be supportive and give service any way you can.
It doesn't matter what you do in your daily life. Simply ask the
question, "how can I serve?" Then surrender to the outcome.
Embrace the moment to help someone.
I get thousands of moments like these at my job in retail.
They may be tiny moments, but they bring me great joy.
I get even greater moments like these when I share
my writing. When people enjoy my words.
I may never be a Dr. D., but I feel my joy, my bliss, my
purpose in my life, and Love these moments.
I am so Grateful for *"The Shift."*
I will never forget him.

I Saw an Angel Today

Her book cover is a rainbow heart.
How can I not be attracted? Rainbows and hearts.
The title is empowering and unbelievable.
If you are not suffering from a bodily illness, you probably can
heal from the mental and emotional conditions in your life.
I am attracted to her story. Not just her personal story but
about her professional story as an author and a publisher.
Her personal story is all too familiar for so many women.
To take that experience, heal from it and then teach
millions of others to heal themselves is amazing.
She talks about the power of thought and offers
affirmations to transcend the thoughts.
She talks about healthy eating and healthy living.
After rewriting her pamphlet into her now famous book, she
decided to self publish her creation which then became a publishing
company with over one hundred and thirty authors.
I wish there was a count of how many lives she has touched
and even saved, with over forty million copies of her book
sold, and the countless support groups she has held.
Not to mention all the conferences, books and
radio shows she continues to produce.
Her talents go beyond the imagination, and one only needs to
look her up to then be flooded with more information.
My life has been touched by her works in more ways than I can remember,
and that rainbow heart book is exactly what I needed at the time.
My dream is to meet her in person.
To look her in the eyes, give her a hug, and say Thank-you.
I will never forget her.

I Saw an Angel Today

My personal Spiritual Guru's graciously agreed to be my
youngest son's God parents and have fulfilled the position to
it's entirety. Offering spiritual knowledge beyond words.
I have also received the benefits of his lessons through
reading the many books they offered on birthdays and
Christmas's, and sometimes even just a visit.
Most of the books received were written by a wonderful
couple who have perfected the art of channelling and
recording the teachings of a group of spiritual beings.
Of the many books we have read from these authors,
the ones I enjoyed the most were about a little girl who
speaks with an ethereal owl named Solomon.
It reminded me of when I was young and had so
many questions about life, God, and heaven.
The little girl in this series is learning about the *Law of
Attraction* through adventures with her friends.
The three books were written for adolescents,
but a definite must read for every-one.
Some "how to" novels for the *Law of Attraction.*
I have enjoyed all the books and audios that this amazing
couple have devoted their life to sharing with us.
I highly recommend the teachings of *Abraham*.
We all have a spiritual path to find and follow.
Between the books for the children and the books for the
masters, we will find an area of reference perfect for where
we are in our own spiritual and personal growth.
I am so very Grateful for the gifts of love from my son's Godparents
and the authors of these amazing spiritual lessons.
I will never forget them.

I Saw an Angel Today

She is hosting another program that feeds my soul.
Now she interviews people who have amazing spiritual
experiences, lessons, and stories of Love to share.
Last night I came home feeling very defeated from my day
at work and the challenges of a corporate restructure.
I was feeling like I had no clue what the purpose of this job
is and that there must be something better to do.
It was like some-one had knocked me down and
then kicked me a few hundred times.
It hurts me and my family when I bring that home.
It was time to gather our dinner and sit down to watch some
of our taped programs. We searched the programs, and there
she was. Like a Super Bowl Sunday for the football fans, she
was helping to refuel, reignite, and renew my soul.
I immediately felt lighter and full.
She seemed to ask all the right questions that received just
the right answers for what I was needing to hear.
The show got paused many times as the program also
sparked conversations between my partner and I.
Our favorite times together. Talking about Love, abundance,
acceptance, self worth, giving, receiving, and serving.
I am so Grateful that one of my favorite ladies in the talk
show world has chosen to do these types of interviews.
I look forward to all her programs on her OWN network.
I hope she knows and feels how she changes lives.
How she changed my outlook and my day.
How she touches my heart.
I will never forget her.

I Saw an Angel Today

I see him everywhere and he always makes me smile.
He is usually in the form of a statue and he is always
smiling or laughing. A joyful happy face.
He is sometimes holding prayer beads and almost always has
a cloth sack near him. His name means "cloth sack."
He has many names, but his face and body are recognized
around the world and in many different cultures.
Some say he is a God of happiness, abundance, wisdom, and contentment.
Some say he is the future embodiment of one of
the fourth largest religions of the world.
Some confuse him with the founder of the religion his
name sounds like, yet the spelling is different as well as
the areas of the world he is most recognized.
I am just attracted to his laughing, joyful, happy face.
I believe that he represents Gratitude.
He seems to always be giving what little he has,
and it seems to make him very happy.
He appears to be very content and wise.
Like a crazy old wise professor, he seems to hold
the knowledge of wealth and abundance.
Some say that if you rub his belly it brings
wealth, good luck, and prosperity.
I think that he has messages to bring to those open to it.
I know that when I see him I have a more open and giving
heart. I feel happy and almost always laugh out loud.
I always want to rub his belly but feel silly doing it.
I should get a statue for my own home to do just that.
I will never forget him.

I Saw an Angel Today

I get messages from him every morning.
It always amazes me that the messages seem to be exactly
what I need in the moments I receive them.
His lessons are that *Thoughts Create Things*, choose the
good ones and create *Totally Unique Thoughts*.
I have been to his website and studied up on who he is and
where he came from, because it always amazes me that
his insights are so clear. Like messages from God.
He had an amazing life that led him to where he is today.
He was a successful accountant and tax advisor.
He then decided to create a family t-shirt business.
One million t-shirts and ten years later he created a club of *Life
Adventurers* which now has over seven hundred thousand members.
I, being one of them, receive a daily message of Love, hope,
encouragement, excitement, understanding, and joy.
He has become an amazing author with millions of books
sold. Not bad for a guy that admits he is not a reader.
Along with his books, and many others he recommends,
he offers, calendars, greeting cards and world tours.
He and his adventurers travel to some of the most amazing areas on
the planet and create a spiritual communion at the same time.
My dream is to join him on one of these amazing trips. To share
with him our love for the wonders of our planet, the adventures
in those areas, and to come together with like minds.
A trip of a lifetime.
I look forward to the messages I receive every day.
I look forward to his recommendations for many things.
I will never forget him.

I Saw an Angel Today

At the age of two he passed all tests given to him and was
recognized as the fourteenth incarnate Spiritual Leader of Tibet.
Fifteen years before I was born and on his fifteenth year
of his young life, he assumed full temporal duties.
Nine years later there was an uprising that had him
flee to India, where he lives today as a refugee.
He is a very inquisitive man and has a wealth of knowledge.
He continues to study constantly, and always stays in
tune with what is happening around the World.
He appears to spend most of his time giving public
speeches and interviews. He continues to teach Buddhism
to large public audiences all over the World.
Despite being over eighty years old he has a very busy schedule
with international lectures and teaching events.
Often with over two hundred thousand students at a time.
He speaks to many topics such as the environment, economics,
women's rights, non-violence, interfaith, physics, astronomy,
Buddhism and science, reproductive health, and sexuality.
Due to the use of Social Networks, it is easy to follow
him, listen to him, and learn from him.
He has an amazing sense of humour and one can learn
to be as lighthearted and playful as he is.
He has stated that he may not be reborn again suggesting
that the function of his role may be outdated.
I cannot imagine a world without him.
He is a symbol of peace and non-violence.
He is a symbol of Love, compassion, and forgiveness.
I will never forget him.

I Saw an Angel Today

Another book has practically jumped off the book shelf
and into my hands. I love when that happens.
On the Top Ten List in 1995, I still share the information
with family and friends looking for spiritual direction.
The Seven Spiritual Laws are still the foundation to
a happy, fulfilling, creative and abundant life.
The author is one of my favorite warriors of the
New Age Enlightenment Movement.
He has a history and a future that creates a lot of criticism
from his own medical and scientific brothers and sisters.
He believes a person can attain perfect health free from
disease and pain, with a body that cannot age or die.
He sees the body as energy and information and not just matter. An
interesting alternative medicine called Ayurveda or "Life Knowledge."
He says that the Universe is like a reality sandwich with
three layers. *The Material World*, *Quantum Zone*, and a
Virtual Zone. And that we are all hard wired to God.
Some of the information I saw from him today is quite
advanced for my simplistic approach to my spiritual life.
For some of his millions of followers, it is the only way.
I still have the little book that jumped off the shelf
and guides me on my spiritual path.
I practice *The Laws* every chance I get and at every opportunity that arises.
I am Grateful that he was one of my spiritual
guru's who led me to where I am today.
I will never forget him.

I Saw an Angel Today

She wakes up creating mental lists of all she is Grateful for.
She starts her day thinking she only wants to sit and write.
She tries to get the morning chores out of the way so that
maybe she has time to jot some of these thoughts down.
She breathes deeply and asks for guidance in all that she does, with all the
people she encounters, and in all the opportunities to be of service today.
She goes to work and tries to smile and help people during
her everyday responsibilities at her paying job.
Wishing she could do more. Wishing for more time, money,
and resources to accomplish more Angel services.
She sees the need for help in so many faces.
She takes solace in knowing that each small little opportunity
always arises, and it is all perfectly timed.
Today, she wasn't sure why she was at work.
It is her day off and she had a thousand other things to do.
Along came another lady that was supposed to be on holidays,
apparently needing to talk to somebody about her "stuff."
She listened and offered some solutions.
She spoke from years of similar experiences.
They both left feeling lighter and brighter.
I smiled and went to the washroom before I left.
I am still smiling as I wash my hands and give thanks.
I swear I see the outlines of wings in the mirror.
I realize I am, who I seek everyday.
An Angel Today.
Every-day.

Celebrity Angels

I saw an Angel Today

She is one of the bravest ladies I have ever heard of.
She has taken a form of communication and has
conquered the prejudices of many.
She has a daytime talk show and addresses the interests
of the masses, but always takes it a step further.
Through the hundreds of shows I have seen, she always
appears to turn negative topics into positive information for
everyone's benefit. Positive outcomes. Positive energy.
She uses her platform for introducing some new ways of
approaching old topics. She has helped nations in the growth
of their minds bodies and spiritual connections.
She not only talks her talk, I belief she walks her walk.
An amazing investigative mind. She has not only gathered
the information but seems to have given every topic a try
herself so that she is not misguiding or misinforming her
audience. Seemingly becoming an expert about the topic.
Thousands of viewers, millions of followers.
A big responsibility, she appears to master.
So many lives she has touched. So many smiles, tears, giggles,
and even anger that she has addressed for so many.
She is probably responsible for some serious life changes.
She even talks about Angels and good deeds as she is the
life embodiment of what she is trying to teach us.
Her smile, her glow, and her life, has become a household name.
A face, a name, a network.
Her *OWN* legacy.
Everyone knows her.
I will never forget her.

I Saw an Angel Today

He is standing on a stage talking to thousands of teens.
Ultimately millions of viewers.
He is accepting an award for something, but his
speech is one I hope everyone gets to see.
He talks about "the industry" and how it works.
He explains that he feels like a fraud.
He talks about his life and how he started working as roofer with
his dad and then all the things that led him to where he is today.
He talks about how he has never had a job that he was
better than. That he was just lucky to have a job.
How he never quit his job before he had his next job.
How opportunity looks a lot like work.
He talks about how being sexy is being "really
smart, thoughtful and generous."
He talks about how we are programmed to think that
we need to be a certain way to have a life.
That everything we see around us, was made by people no smarter than us.
He is telling them that they can build their own **thing**. Their own life.
He ends his speech by saying "So build a life, don't live one."
"Build a Life, find your opportunity, and always be sexy!"
He points to his head as he says to "always be sexy."
I am so happy that he has used this platform and has
given this speech to the next generation.
I am so Grateful.
I need to share his speech with everyone.
I will never forget him.

I Saw an Angel Today

She is trying to smile though everyone knows
she is not happy in her current life.
Everyone knows she needs to get out.
To get away from this family of stature.
She has the biggest heart and the good will of a saint.
She uses her status to bring awareness to the world
and help the needy anyway she can.
She travels and makes appearances to places no-
one in her home would dream of visiting.
She does this to educate the world about the lives of other
people who live in less fortunate areas of our planet.
She is loved and adored around the World.
This appears to be the only love she gets in her
life except for that of her two sons.
Her smiles are filled with joy and love when she
is with them. They are her world.
She is so proud and playful with them.
She doesn't seem to care who is watching.
We are all watching.
We don't have a choice.
They plaster her pictures and her life all over the T.V.
and news stands. A lot of it untrue, I am sure.
Today, the picture on the front of the magazine said that her husband
is cheating with the woman he should have originally married.
While they show pictures of her playing with her
children, they sell magazines with this headline.
She will handle this with the grace of a Princess.
I will never forget her.

I Saw an Angel Today

I have been watching him most of my life.
He is the most talented person I have ever seen.
His talents range from singing and song writing to acting and producing.
If you listen, really listen, he has a lot to say.
His heart appears as big as his life.
His songs are used to raise awareness and funds
to help people in need, globally.
He writes about Love, acceptance, honor, and respect.
His messages are converted into movements of dance
that can create hysteria in about three steps.
Especially if he performs them.
He has created a revolution of music, dance, fashion, and
awareness that will go down in the history books.
He has the respect of millions but also the judgement of
thousands who do not understand his way of thinking.
He is being accused of horrific crimes against
what he loves the most. The children.
Those who love him unconditionally will only believe
the innocent child within him and his story.
His talents and messages are all too soon forgotten as
he gets lost in the drama of the accusations.
He is trying to please the World at the expense of himself and
who he is. He appears to be a lost boy in *Neverland*.
He teaches me to look at the person in the mirror, to honor
and respect all races, and to have a charitable heart.
When I hear his voice, it is impossible for me not to sing.
To dance, to smile, and to remember.
I will never forget him.

I Saw an Angel Today

It's her Birthday, but she won't be blowing out any candles.
She has received her wings and is no longer with us.
She has powerful messages, and everyone is honoring her,
on this day that she would have been sixteen.
She was the girl next door and seemed to have the
life most girls her age can only dream of.
She may no longer be on the physical planet, but she is
very much alive in thousands of people's hearts.
She was bullied and extorted to death, but through
her story she has helped so many.
Probably will continue to help millions.
She posted an online video that is going viral.
It was just her story on pieces of paper that she held up.
Story of being blackmailed and extorted and then bullied.
Physically bullied then cyber-bullied when she could no
longer go to school. Two different schools, as she tried
to get away from the rumours and the pain.
She developed mental health issues and although she had all
the help and programs available to her and her family, she
decided to leave us on Mental Health Awareness Day.
She probably thought no-one loved her or cared
about her and that she meant nothing.
I know she is still with us and working.
Working to save other kids lives with her story.
Helping to educate and guide families in crisis, helping them to *Stay Strong*.
Her legacy may live forever.
I am so proud and Grateful to be part of creating it.
I will never forget her.

I Saw an Angel Today

He has released a documentary just before a presidential
election that hopefully, will not be forgotten.
He is speaking about climate changes.
He went on a tour for two years all over our great planet and
has filmed the effects of the last fifteen to twenty years.
It is hard to believe that anyone can deny the obvious
changes in our climate and the devastating results.
He is taking his position of Ambassador of Climate Change
very seriously and works hard to educate society on global
warming and the consequences of our actions.
He has wrapped his life around these issues, and yet some
how finds the time to act in many great films.
In his latest film they had to relocate half way around the
world to find enough snow for many of the scenes.
He is also involved in many charities and environmental
groups and donates millions to these causes.
He tries to leave a very small environment foot print in his daily
life and receives a lot of bad publicity if his actions don't.
I am in awe at his bravery.
I am Grateful for his ability to reach the masses and
to create a platform of positive changes.
I am filled with hope as he finishes this film with the
positive changes already occurring around the world.
My hope for Humanity.
Our Messenger of Peace seems to only be asking that we pay attention
Before the Flood and help to make the small changes to preserve this
planet for our children, our grandchildren, and the generations to come.
I will never forget him.

I Saw an Angel Today

She loves to make people laugh and dance.
It appears that that she loves to scare people more.
I am surprised she gets any celebrity guests agreeing to visit
her for fear of getting scared silly in front of millions.
Most of her interviews are the feel-good stories about people
making positive changes in other people's lives.
I am realizing that I have never watched her do an
interview or a story without a positive outcome.
She introduces her audience to all those Angels I love to
write about. Those people like her, making changes.
Changes to our planet, our cultures, our life styles,
and to each other. People helping people.
She has the most amazing heart and she gives fully from it.
She has helped make some massive changes in peoples lives by
giving them gifts to help them in many different situations.
She appears to have hundreds of sponsors in her back pocket as she
gives away money, grants, computers, and even cars to help people
with their Angel endeavours. Programs that help even more people.
Above all of this, she is still one of those brave women who speaks openly
about her sexual orientation and has probably helped thousands of others
be true to themselves. Be free to Love whoever they choose to Love.
She easily drives home the messages of Universal Love.
Today, I watched as a guest described her in these words;
She loves to get people excited, which helps them to feel
great and then they are more than happy to *Be Kind to
One Another*, and to just *Have a Little Fun Today*.
I will never forget her.

I Saw an Angel Today

I am proud that he comes from my country and even
from the same school as some of my friends.
He is an actor, author, producer, and activist.
I grew up watching him on TV and the big screen.
My children still own his trilogy about a car made into a
time machine and the effects of messing with time.
He was a teen idol and a household name.
Now he is the face of a fighter of an incurable disease.
He battles symptoms of Parkinson's Disease and has
made a cure for it his focus and priority.
He believes he will see the cure in his lifetime.
He has written a book about his life, the discovery of his
illness and how he has grown and learned from it.
I believe that his support system through his wife and family
helps keep him strong and passionate about a cure.
I admire his bravery and his strength.
I know from my own life experience what dealing with
constant pain and discomfort does to a loved one.
I believe he has a message and a life purpose to share.
I think he is so much more than this disease.
He is one of the most talented actors of my time.
He has been one of the main characters in many
of my favorite movies and TV shows.
He is a local hero and they have named a theatre after him.
I hope he is remembered for all the things he has done
that he loves to do, and not just for this disease.
Although, if his Foundation found the cure, he
would be most proud of that, I am sure.
I will never forget him.

I Saw an Angel Today

She is bringing awareness to the realities of a very large
religious order that many have wondered about for years.
She is very brave as I believe they could be very dangerous.
She grew up with this organization and for the
longest time she sang their praises.
She is an actress, so they used her to gain an audience.
Now I am sure that they wish they had kept her quiet.
I am sure they wish they knew how to silence her.
It is now her passion to find and interview people
who have managed to leave the organization.
The stories she has uncovered about families torn
apart and lives ruined, has been unbelievable.
I am heart broken about some of the things
that have happened to these people.
I knew a girl many years ago that was banned from her
own family and it tore her heart apart at every event.
It amazes me that these organizations call themselves a church.
It diminishes the meaning of the word.
I believe that everyone has a right to choose any belief
they want to follow, as long as no-one gets hurt.
There are many forms of abuse these places are
responsible for. Mostly mental cruelty.
Then along comes this brave little Angel.
She calls herself a *Troublemaker*.
I am hoping and praying that God keeps her safe.
I am also hoping her information can be used to shut down
this kind of business that is nothing more than a cult.
I am Grateful for Angels like her.
I will never forget her.

I Saw an Angel Today

He portrayed an alien on TV when I was little.
His characters were often full of life and laughs.
The roles I loved him in the most was when he was playing
with some dolphins or with a gorilla named KoKo.
He was bringing awareness to the animal kingdom.
Through those documentaries you saw a Love in
him that surpasses this reality, this realm.
He played with these creatures with the Love and excitement
of a child experiencing joy for the first time.
He was just as interested in learning about them
as they were, learning about him.
They took time to touch and hug, look into each others'
eyes, and appreciate each others' energy.
That was a profound message for me. A message of Love.
Actions that speak louder than words.
Respect given and received.
Today, I have learned that he decided to leave his earthly
body and in doing so, he left messages for other people.
He was battling a mental illness that others are not yet fully
aware of. A condition called Lewy Body Dementia.
He was aware of the stress that this would put on his
family, and it appeared he didn't want to burden them.
I hope the World learns more from his illness.
I have learned to Love and accept Love, even from an alien.
I have learned that even though we appear to be
different, in so many ways we are all the same.
NaNoo, NaNoo my hero.
Thanks for the giggles and smiles.
I will never forget you.

I Saw an Angel Today

My family always jokes that when something seems a little
weird and unordinary, there was a glitch in *The Matrix*.
Years later I learned that 70% of this Angel's earnings
from these amazing movies, was donated to others.
Many of his movies have left me thinking about
alternate realities and the human spirit.
I have also learned of the many life lessons he has lived
through. It appears he gained mountains of strength through
his own life challenges, and he continues to help others.
He is known to stop and help a stranded motorist, and
even stand in line at one of his own events.
He supports many charities and gives freely of his own time
and energy. Thirteen charities and fifteen Causes.
It is said that he is the only Hollywood star without a
mansion, and that he still prefers to ride the subway.
They say that he is one of the most down to earth celebrities
of all time. A quiet soul with a ton of wisdom.
Some have said that he is the nicest celebrity to work with.
Often treating the film crews to breakfast and speaking to
them with genuine interest. Full of human kindness.
When asked if he was a spiritual person, he replied with: "I don't
know? I don't know the spiritual Richter-scale measurement! That's a
weird answer, isn't it? I don't know." "Do I believe in God, faith, inner
faith, the self, passion, and things? Yes, of course! I'm very spiritual ...
supremely spiritual ... bountifully spiritual ... supremely bountiful."
His name means "gentle breeze over the mountains".
I will never forget him.

I Saw an Angel Today

I have always thought of her as one of the most beautiful
women in the world. Many media outlets report the same.
She appears to spend most of her time travelling to
conflict torn countries and working with refugees.
She has become the face and voice for the children and
women of these areas. A *Refugee Guardian Angel*.
She has created villages with medical facilities, schools,
and factories for families to make a living.
She has also funded large animal conservation projects
resulting in more protected areas and more villages.
She works within her home country to try to change legislation
that will aid unaccompanied child immigrants.
She has a team of lawyers working in *KIND*.
She has received many awards for her humanitarian work.
She was even appointed Honorary Dame Commander
of the Order of St. Michael and St. George.
I am sure she has changed the lives of countless families, including her own.
She has six children and three of them were adopted internationally.
She appears to be very passionate about teaching them where they
are from and how they can make a difference. Naming a few of these
Foundations after two of her children and including them in their efforts.
Although there have been reports of a troubling personal
life, she seems to have the fight of a heroine in her.
If one minces words just a little, her name would be....
Angel of Joy.
I am so Grateful she has not forgotten about the children.
I will never forget her.

I Saw an Angel Today

Growing up in a family of four women, he was the
heart throb we would all swoon over.
He has matured and grown grey more handsomely
than anyone else on the big screen.
He has the most recognized eyes and crooked little smile.
I remember when he was named the "Sexiest Man Alive".
Today, it appears his passion is about fighting for
the rights of others around the World.
His biggest fight is for the human rights in Tibet.
When he was in his twenties, he found interest in Buddhism
and studied Zen Buddhism for five or six years.
He eventually met the fourteenth Dalai Lama in India
and became a practicing Tibetan Buddhist.
Due to his outspoken political views, he is banned from
a country with strong influence in his industry.
Embracing his apparent exile, he has focused on the independent
arena and has produced some of the best reviews of his career.
He supports Survivor International which helps protect the
rights and lands of tribal people around the World.
He also campaigns for ecological causes and AIDS awareness,
especially for women and children in India.
He works with supporting global initiatives to
promote peace, justice, and understanding.
I think his passion and work may be best explained through some of
his writings in "We Are One: A Celebration of Tribal Peoples."
I loved him on the big screen. I Love who he is today.
I will never forget him.

I Saw an Angel Today

He is an actor, filmmaker, and political activist.
Not an easy thing to do in his industry.
Others prefer to keep their heads down and not have an opinion
on politics for fear of loosing popularity and work.
He has been very vocal on his stand against war
and violence as well as other hot topics.
He even placed a $56,000 open letter advertisement
asking to end a cycle of violence, referring to the planned
attack on Iraq and the so called, "War on Terror."
He appears to believe, as I do, that you cannot stop violence
with violence. That war should never even be considered.
He has been very actively involved in relief efforts after
some of the most disastrous events of our times.
He founded the J/P Haitian Relief Organization and
was named Ambassador-at-Large for Haiti.
A place close to my heart as the disaster occurred while I
was on the other side of the Island. A second home.
He has even visited the villages of the flood-stricken areas of
Pakistan to hand out blankets and supplies to survivors.
He has been vocal on his support of same-sex marriage
saying, "We've got to have equal rights for every-one!"
He has been active in trying to open dialogue between conflicting countries
offering that "communication is the only way to achieve a better solution."
I think he is one of the bravest men I have ever seen.
I think he brings awareness and clarity to many political
situations and offers peace as a better way of living.
I also feel that action speaks louder than words.
I will never forget him.

I Saw an Angel Today

There are so many of them involved in the biggest big
brother protection watch I have ever heard of.
They have founded and funded some of the most amazing
projects and systems for watching over the people in areas
around the World with mass atrocities to human rights.
They bring awareness and provide rapid response systems
to areas that needed and continue to need assistance.
They enlist the support of artists, activists, and cultural leaders
to raise awareness of the activities in these areas.
One of the projects they worked closely with and funded was a launch of
a satellite system that watched over the people, virtually protecting them.
SSP detected quite a few mass grave sites that were
freshly dug and provided the information required to stop
the horrific actions before they could get started.
As I read up on all these projects that seem to link together,
I started recognizing the thousands of other Angels involved.
A massive amount of them working together.
I am realizing that although there are many famous faces
attached to some of the most amazing projects, there are
millions of helper Angels along side of them.
Like the Arch Angels enlist the help of thousands of
Guardian Angels, so do the human Angels.
The human Angels that answer the phones, take the dictation, arrange
the events, work on the technology, study the data, write the reports, and
do thousands of other tasks that help make these programs succeed.
So, as I give thanks for all the big-name Angels,
I will never forget the ones who help them.

Musical Angels

I Saw an Angel Today

I have been hearing a lot of his songs lately.
All his music sends thousands of memories flooding in.
He was my teenage heart throb and I had posters of
him plastered all over my bedroom walls.
He had blonde hair and dark eyes and the most amazing
smile, but his accent melted my heart.
He has three very famous brothers who sing as beautifully
as he does. He gave them all the credit for his success.
I read many articles that spoke of the family Love that the
brothers all shared and how much they loved to be together.
Loved to just be brothers, hanging out and having fun.
Today I watched old music videos to remember him.
I wondered why he seemed so sad and lonely in
his last years in the physical World.
I know he died of a broken heart although he tried
so hard to tell the World he was fine.
There were talk of addictions and depression.
I prefer to remember that sparkle he had.
I remember how the girls in the 1970's would scream and
cry as soon as walked on a stage or opened his mouth.
I am sure there are many women out there that only need
to hear, "For so Long," and they break into song.
When I think of his life and the songs that come so
easily to my mind, one song stands out the most.
Although his brothers wrote and produced it, I didn't know
it at the time, but it seemed to be his Big Finale.
So, dear heart, "How do you Mend a Broken Heart?"
Just with time and by falling in Love again.
I will never forget him.

I Saw an Angel Today

He was in my dream.
I was walking around this massive ranch filled
with horses and people and equipment.
I felt like I knew where I was going.
I walked along a fence line watching the horses run.
It was a warm sunny day but there were still bits of snow
around. Was it Spring or Fall? I wasn't sure.
I kept walking along and turned down a path between
two buildings. I smiled at a man shoeing a horse.
I turned right when the buildings ended and came out into
the open again. I looked up at the beautiful mountains.
I heard some music and followed the sound.
I turned right again and found him. I smiled.
He was sitting on some steps with his guitar in hand and there
were quite a few children sitting on the ground listening to him.
I listened for awhile and felt so peaceful.
He turned to look at me and smiled.
I felt warm and thought the sun was shining on my face.
I turned away not wanting to disturb him and the kids.
I awoke from my dream and wondered why I was dreaming
of this fellow. I don't know him personally.
A few days later, I found out that he had passed.
He was my first introduction to country music and maybe
the reason the mountains are always calling to me.
Whenever I head out of the city towards the Rockies I love so
much, I am always singing "Take Me Home Country Roads."
His music will always be a part of my life.
I will never forget him.

I Saw an Angel Today

I was so proud and amazed at her voice.
When and how did she learn to do that?
I remembered her singing in the kitchen when we were growing up,
but never like that. We used to tease her and tell her to hush.
She sounded like one of those *Ladies of Country Music*.
One of the ladies that she had always loved to listen to.
She was even playing guitar.
She was playing guitar and singing on a stage.
A small stage in a small place but there she was.
She had obviously been learning, practicing, and
working hard at that new life she had created.
She seemed so happy to be performing for me.
She appeared to be performing just for me.
I guess it's not too often you get to show your
child that very talented side of yourself.
That side of yourself that others see but your kids don't.
I hope she saw how proud I was of her.
She smiled at me like she just read my thoughts.
I couldn't wait for them to take a break, so I could hug her.
I never thought it was possible to be so proud of your mother.
She finished a song and then announced that the next one was for
her daughter. She started to play and then she sang one word.
"Crazy." My eyes filled with tears.
My heart swelled, and I was choked up with pride.
She sounded like the famous lady who recorded it.
I was amazed and still kind of in shock.
I now know where my Love of singing came from.
Now that she has her wings, I wish I had a recording of that night.
I will never forget her.

I Saw an Angel Today

There are two of them. They are sisters but have different styles
of singing and they are both famous in their own stage lights.
They both have me hooked on country music and I know
almost every word to all their most famous hits.
They were born in the coal mine towns of Kentucky and
they both sings songs from that time of their lives.
Most women can relate to the lyrics in their songs, in different stages
of their lives, or with different ways of handling personal situations.
One of them sings about being a strong woman with "You
Ain't Woman Enough to Take My Man," while the other sings
about how a man can "Make Your Brown Eyes Blue."
One of the sisters in considered more of a pop singer, but
she has earned her places on the country charts.
As the two women are nineteen years apart, one was
more famous in the sixty's and seventies, while the other
was more famous in the eighties and nineties.
Both women have helped me through some of the most
difficult times of my life, some of the happiest times, and
a lot of the times when a girl just has to sing.
They both played a huge part in my love for the mountains, as
I sing along to "Rocky Top" and "Coal Miners Daughter."
Though everyone has different styles of music they love, at different
times of their lives, these two ladies are my go to "good ol' hits."
The ones that come out from the back of the drawers, depending
on my mood and what is going on for me at the time.
I think of them when I want to sing.
I am Grateful for their talents.
I will never forget them.

I Saw an Angel Today

I received the call while I was in the mountains camping
with my mother, my sister, and my youngest son.
The World has lost another King.
This one was the "King of Pop" music.
I was one of his biggest fans.
I have collected tons of memorabilia over the years.
He was the one musician most of my family appreciated.
It was apparently an accidental overdose.
I felt in my heart that he was finally free.
He was finally free from the media, the critics, and the demands
of the business that seemed to take its toll on him.
They said he was working on another World tour.
I would have waited in line all night for tickets like I did twenty
years ago. I was so excited he was performing again.
In my heart he was the World's greatest performer.
I got teased a lot for being one of his billions of followers.
I was heart broken when I got the news.
I was sad for his kids, who will have to grow up without their
very talented father. I think he was creating this tour for them.
He never would have wanted to leave his children to grow up the
way he had to. With the media at their door steps constantly.
When he was passing, he probably thought he was flying
like Peter Pan. Something he always wanted to do.
There will be so much media coverage over the next few weeks.
I am Grateful I am in the mountains away from it all.
Time to reflect and just listen to his music.
Remember a Time, a legend, a *Thriller*.
I will never forget him.

I Saw an Angel Today

For as long as I can remember, her music has been part of
my growing up years, and my own children's lives.
We used to hurry to get our baths done, pajamas on, and
lay in a line on the floor in front of the television.
As the camera flies over the mountain top meadows, and you
see her start to twirl in a circle, you just have to sing.
You only need to speak the words, "The hills are alive"
and people will know exactly what to say next.
Sometimes when I want to focus on more positive things in
my life, I will start singing "My Favorite Things" and then
"I don't feel so bad." In fact, I am filled with joy.
One of my fondest memories is when my oldest was going
through a stage of asking me "why?" after everything I said. The
only way to get him to stop asking why, was when I would say,
"Because, supercalifragilisticexpialidocious!" He would look at me
with interest and then just say "OK" and then walk away.
Today, I found that there is so much more to this
amazingly talented lady than her songs, her movies, and
her Broadway performances and directing talents.
She has a passion for Children Literacy and has co-written
around twenty children's books with her daughter.
She is a Good Will Ambassador to the UN, bringing
attention to abused women around the World.
She is also a board member of Operation USA, helping
children and families in times of disasters.
Dubbed Dame Commander by the Queen, she has
most definitely made her mark on the World.
I may not have had a nanny like Mary Poppins,
but I will never forget her!

I Saw an Angel Today

There are two of them and they sing like Angels.
Over the years I have learned every word to every one of
their songs, and later, the solo songs of the daughter's.
It was one of the most brilliant ideas that her momma
had, creating this mother and daughter duo.
Going from living on welfare in California, returning home to Tennessee,
and then creating a $30 demo tape that she desperately tried to promote.
Momma was often met with propositions, sexual harassment,
and prompt dismissals, while trying to promote their music.
She studied to become a nurse and after caring for a record
producer's daughter, she convinced him to come to their home
and listen to the act. He was sold. They were signed.
They had twenty-five singles on the charts in seventeen
years. Fourteen went to number one and six more was
on the Top Ten lists. I own every one of them.
They won five Grammy Awards, and eight CMA Awards.
They had so many wonderful music videos, but by far
my favorite was "Love can Build a Bridge."
I was devastated when I learned that the duo would
not be a duo anymore, so that Momma could stay home
and take care of herself and her health issues.
I watched and cried as they performed at the *Farewell
Concert*. The daughter seemed so scared and alone as
she realized she had to learn to soar on her own.
I always think of my own *Grampa* when I hear the song.
I get tears in my eyes when I hear, "Momma I found someone, like you
said would come along" as I have lost my own Momma not too long ago.
Sometimes I can't remember what I did last night, but I
can recite every lyric to every one of their songs.
I will never forget them.

I Saw an Angel Today

I heard he was coming to town to perform one of
his amazing concerts everyone talks about.
When a big name like his comes to perform, you start
speed dialing, trying to get tickets over the phone.
The concert sold out in several minutes.
I missed it. Crushed I walked away from the phone.
The radio announced a second concert.
I rushed back to the phone. It sold out even faster.
I missed it again.
A third concert was announced, and I missed that one too.
I was determined not to miss his show, so my sister and I
went down to the Dome and looked for a ticket scalper.
As we stood there, the box office window opened, and they sold some
tickets. We thought that it was for something else, so we didn't get in line.
Then we noticed the excited people going through the doors with
their new tickets, so we waited for the window to open again.
Amazingly it did, and we paid bottom dollar for floor seats.
We felt like we won the lottery.
We decided to sit at the far back until the show started.
A big bouncer fellow came to us and said, "These look like
pretty lousy seats and maybe these ones would be better?"
Front row, Center stage.
It was the best show I have ever seen. Country meets Rock.
We have since learned that this Angel keeps adding shows and a
slow release of tickets to hurt the scalping business, but mainly for
his fans. He believes the fans are more important than anything.
I will never miss *The Dance* and anxiously wait for him to
return. One of the greatest performers I have ever seen.
I will never forget him.

I Saw an Angel Today

For some reason my Mom loved to bug me about
being one of this lady's biggest fans.
She would sing a line from one of her songs and
drawl it out to the point of being silly.
I cannot remember how I came to love her music.
All I do remember is that she always seemed to be there.
In the background, in the car, in my Walkman, then my
Discman. Through my laughter and my tears.
I cannot decorate the Christmas tree without her
Christmas album playing along with us.
She is definitely one of the Queens of Country Music
and I own every one of her albums, now CD's.
She is an amazing actress and I have seen every episode of
her TV series about a single mom with three kids.
She started another one when the first one ended
but unfortunately it didn't last very long.
In my mind I have seen thousands of her movies, forgetting
that almost everyone of her music videos is a mini-movie.
She seems to love acting as much as singing.
I have probably seen every movie she has performed in,
but my favorite is when she played Annie Oakley.
She seems to have a pretty private personal life, even when she
married her manager and more recently when they divorced.
She still seems to have it all together.
She is one of my biggest hero's in music.
Today, and every-time I listen to "Cathy's Clown," since
my mother got her wings, I cry. Just another one of
those life memories she has been a huge part of.
I will never forget her.

I Saw an Angel Today

They were the British Invasion in our music history.
Four amazingly talented young men.
Named the "Fab Four" they were the best-selling band with
over eight hundred million physical and digital albums.
They were the influential act of the Rock era.
After arriving in the USA, they gave their first live US
television performance that was watched by over seventy-
three million viewers or 34% of the population.
They were an unstoppable song writing team of the 1960's
and ahead of their time with social messages.
Described as an "Embodiment of social cultural movements of the decade,"
they became catalysts for activism in social and political arenas.
Their songs and styles began fuelling movements for
women's rights, gay liberation, and environmentalism.
After an anti-religious comment nearly destroyed their
popularity, they put more effort into their lyrics that helped to
spread messages of higher consciousness and wisdom.
I have a funny story that I like to share, about not even really
knowing who they were, as I am such a country music girl.
As I develop my awareness of messages received in all forms of our senses,
I am awestruck by the lyrics of this amazing and talented group of artists.
They may have only been together for ten years, but
their musical style and songs will go on forever.
They all went on to deliver even more amazing work
under their individual names and styles.
I Love to listen to all their lyrics with an open heart.
I will never forget them.

I Saw an Angel Today

Her music came into my life as I was rediscovering who I am and why
things never seemed to work out right in my romantic relationships.
I am sure that was the case for so many others.
I fell in Love with her instantly when I listened
to her lyrics and then read her book.
I really wanted to understand how hard it must have
been for a singer/songwriter to be "out."
After learning her story and becoming more comfortable in
my own *Skin*, I realized she is just one of the most amazing
singers, and a hero of women in Rock & Roll.
One of the greatest pieces of work she has done since my discovery of
her amazing songs, is a song and video called "I Need to Wake Up."
Written for a documentary called An Inconvenient Truth.
Even in her music video of the song, the message of how we all need to
take responsibility for our planet is driven home, and hard to ignore.
She has delivered so many great messages through her music in the past,
but I never get tired of listening to and watching this one particular video.
I may not have known anything about this amazing Earth
Angel in the years when I needed her in my young love
life, but I am forever Grateful to have found her.
She is an inspiration with her own personal struggles
and triumphs over the past twenty years.
I will never forget her.

I Saw an Angel Today

He was influenced by a rap singer that was, and still is,
considered to be one of the greatest and most influential
rappers of all time. His hero was also an actor.
I never did understand the East/West Coast Hip Hop Rivalry, but it seemed
to be where he drew his love of lyrics from and where he discovers his beats.
He has a very natural talent, and I always thought he could
have been one of the famous ones. One of the big stars.
He once told me that he never really wanted his songs to be
picked up by any label because his *First Love* would become
a job and not a labour of Love. A favorite past-time.
Almost twenty years later, I still want every-one to hear his
first song. It had an amazing message for our kids.
It was a time in our history when a teenager must have
been terrified of everything going on in the World.
It was a time of too much bad news and not enough good.
It was a time when an impressionable young mind should
have been excited about graduation and a future.
A time when there was no fear except for the natural ones we
all had about being independent and leaving the nest.
They should not have been worried about the World
ending, terrorists, bombs hiding and tainted mail.
We put the "*Weight of the World*" on their minds.
Between the Love of his lyrics and the Love of his God, he
figured it all out and became an amazing husband, father,
friend, son, and our own musical lyric master.
He now has three or four CD's completed.
They are for his family, friends, and a Mom to be proud of.
He is our *Hip Hop Rap Star*.
I could never forget him.

I Saw an Angel Today

He is one of my favorite Canadian Country Singers.
One of the things I enjoy most about him is his very deep voice.
A very recognizable sound when you hear his songs.
Recently I have come to learn so much more
about him and his very big heart.
He now devotes much of his time helping people in need.
I have really enjoyed a show that he is involved with that helps real life
families facing homelessness, build a new home. Then go to another country
where help was needed to build homes, or dig wells, or rebuild a new school.
It is heart warming as I watch a family receive their dream
of having a home of their own, and then the same family
give their hearts away to complete strangers.
Through Love and kindness, every-one is blessed.
The gifts of time, energy, extra hands, and sharing.
The rewards are more than buildings and water.
This Angel had an opportunity to travel to countries
like Cambodia, Ethiopia, Belize, and Uganda and learn
first hand about poverty and homelessness.
He said, "I realized I live in Disneyland here, and
there was something I could do about it."
He launched *Build It Forward* and I pray that it takes
on a life of its own and continues to grow.
I watched a new music video he released called "Give it
Away," and the lyrics are so true for every-one.
I hope someday to be able to travel abroad and give all
that I can through whatever resources I can offer.
We may not be able to do much more than that.
I will never forget him.

I Saw an Angel Today

I have loved his music from the first time I heard it.
Probably because I know his story and I know his heart.
He came into my life indirectly and today I consider
him one of my closest *"True Friends."*
I often call him the big brother I never had.
We have spent countless hours talking about every-
thing under the sun, except his music.
He probably thinks that I am crazy because I have kind
of acted like some sort of groupie over the years.
He has a very unique voice and I love his lyrics.
He puts it all together and the sound is like country music,
blues and folk music was blended on slow speed.
He played with and created a home-grown cassette
that I have cherished over the years.
I had to try to figure out how to get his music into my computer and then
burn it onto a CD before the old cassette snapped from over playing it.
I headed up the mountain and presented him the new CD.
He listened to it like he was hearing it for the first time.
I could see the surprise and wonder in his eyes.
We talked about how the old songs are nearly impossible
to recreate from thirty plus years ago.
We talked about who or what he was thinking when he
wrote his songs and how and where he created them.
From that one little cassette he gave me over twenty-
five years ago, we have created a lasting friendship.
He will never know how many hours I have spent with
him, his memories, his stories, and his music.
I will never forget him.

I Saw an Angel Today

They are all the women and men that have given us their
passion, love, and heart through their music.
They have probably spent most of their lives learning, playing, practicing,
writing, and sharing their deepest thoughts and strongest desires.
They are artists in every sense of the word.
They were brave enough to stick to it and follow their
dreams, working hard to achieve their goals.
Strong enough to keep getting up when they fell or failed.
Passionate enough to learn from their mistakes.
Wise enough to know the outcome of the work.
Lucky enough to be discovered, or not.
I believe if you follow your heart, do what you love to do,
and have a desire to give all you got, you will win.
My life has literally revolved around music.
I cannot remember a minute of my life that music was not
playing in my head. Sometimes like a broken record.
I am so very Grateful for the musicians who have been with
me throughout my life. In good times and in bad.
So many times, when I needed them, they were there.
So many memories. So many loves. So many losses.
They bring us exactly what we need when we need it.
I cannot imagine a world without music.
The language is Universal. The Love is real.
The pitch and rhythm often need no words, but the lyrics
are my messages. Messages from the Universe.
Messages from God and the Angels through all the
Worlds' Musical Earth Angels.
I will never forget them.

Global Events Angels

I Saw an Angel Today

I saw hundreds and maybe thousands today.
There has been a global crisis they are calling 9/11.
There were low energy human beings who have taken a
famous city hostage and has destroyed hundreds of lives.
Have touched the lives of thousands.
There is fire, smoke, crumbling buildings, and dust so
thick people must wear protective gear just to see and
breathe. They can barely see across the streets.
There is fear, anger, tears of sorrow but still hope and
faith, in the trained and untrained Angels scurrying about
helping each other through this horrific day.
BUT, they have not taken our Spirit.
They have strengthened our bond and we have come together
as brothers and sisters taking care of each other.
We are strength in numbers and we are protecting the
innocent, and helping the injured, and consoling the lost.
We are many nations who are strong, united, and
safe in our thoughts, beliefs and in Love.
There are so many everyday people doing Angelic deeds
for complete strangers. Today and tomorrow.
People helping people.
Angels helping Angels.
This was not a day of sorrow for me but a day of remembering
how we came together in our hours of need and conquered
even the most unbelievable circumstances.
Our day
Not theirs.
Our bond of brotherhood and Love.
I will never forget this day.

I saw an Angel Today

She has earned her wings and is finally free.
The world is in mourning, and for the first time in
my life, I can feel the energy of the masses.
Everyone is shocked, and her story seems to be
on every radio and television channel.
Tomorrow it will be all over the papers and the tabloids.
Everyone feels that the paparazzi caused the accident.
Some feel that it was a conspiracy.
I am just trying to remember all the amazing things
she has done for so many people on our planet.
I feel sad for her sons who have been robbed of the years
ahead. Graduation, first girlfriends, marriage, and a family of
their own. She would have loved being a grandmother.
I believe those were her last thoughts, if she had any.
That of her sons and praying they will be alright.
I also think that she would never have wanted people
to remember her by the way she had died.
I believe she would have wanted people to remember that
charity is what you can do, not what you can afford.
I think she would have wanted us to quit judging others
and to offer Love whenever and wherever possible.
I also believe that she would have wanted to tell the world
that people deserve their privacy, no matter who they are.
Finally, I think she would have loved to tell every little girl
that being a **Princess** is not all it's cracked up to be.
Be yourself. Love freely and unconditionally.
But most importantly, Love yourself.
I smile when I think of her smile.
I will never forget her.

I Saw an Angel Today

My son is working on a school project and I am curious.
He must make a presentation about something
that happened in history on his birthday.
It was easy for him to find the World event for that day.
It was a day that changed the World.
A day that thousands of Angels took back their freedom.
He is using special names likes *Operation Neptune*,
Operation Overlord, and *Operation Bodyguard*.
It all sounds scary, exciting, and strong.
One hundred and thirty thousand allied troops had stormed some
beaches in Western Europe and had begun the end of WWII.
Thirty-nine allied divisions and over a million troops came together in the
hour of need and changed the lives of countless men, women, and children.
They were the brave, the strong, and the answers
to thousands of people's prayers.
I am very interested that this operation was very dependant
in the phase of the moon, the tides, and the time of day.
A full moon was most desirable for light.
Many people lost their lives.
More people got their lives back.
Beaches full of Angels.
My son decides to make a music video about the event.
It doesn't take him long as he is passionate about the project
and he can show off his talents and his Love of film.
I wish the World could see his video as I am sure they would learn
more of these amazing facts from our history of Armed Angels.
Even if they are as "anti-war" as the two of us.
We will never forget them.

I Saw an Angel Today

There were seven of them heading for the stars when
a horrific accident occurred killing all of them.
There were two women and five men, and they seemed
to represent the many nations of the world through race,
gender, geographical backgrounds, and religions.
This was probably why so many felt the loss today.
Some people think it was more publicized due to one of the
crew being a female teacher in a special program.
I think that this became a Global Event because it was
filmed, and that a visual story is always more effective.
I am drawn into the stories of them in their personal lives,
as I am relating to the women and their adventure.
I am also wondering how something so scientifically and
so carefully engineered could have just exploded.
I am feeling sad for their families.
I am sure the months, days and years ahead will
reveal something positive about this tragedy.
These are one of those times where you can't help but feel
helpless and that things must have happened for a reason.
It is an opportunity for some people to pray to their
spiritual leaders and for those lost lives.
It brings families and friends closer together as they reflect
on their love of each other and their own blessings.
It is a time for silent thoughts of Gratitude for all the good in
our own lives, and to be thankful for all that we still have.
In a blink of an eye, or seventy-three seconds, we lost
seven amazingly brave, adventurous people.
In seven seconds you can change your feelings around it.
I will never forget them.

I Saw an Angel Today

There are thousands of them hugging and crying and helping each other
with joyful smiles, climb up onto a massive ugly wall with tons of history.
People are celebrating and dancing with complete strangers
in the streets on each side and around this wall.
I have heard reports throughout the morning of the events of
the evening before and wondered what it all means.
Looking at footage from across the ocean, it appears and
feels that a great sense of freedom is in the air.
Where families and friends were torn apart for almost
thirty years, they are finally reunited.
Where people felt isolated and forgotten and longed for a
different and probably better life, the possibility is in sight.
The event seems to mark the beginning of so many
things and the end of so much more.
Everyone appears to have a story about this wall.
What it meant to them and how it feels now.
For days, weeks and years to come, there will be massive
changes to the landscape of this foreign land.
This marks the unification of so many torn apart by
war and by circumstances beyond their control.
I can only imagine what it must feel like to be in
the middle of this celebration of freedom.
I watch as people chip away at this massive wall to
gather a souvenir of what will eventually be gone.
It is wonderful to see the joy and relief in so many faces.
It is amazing what this structure symbolized.
Many lives will change.
I will never forget them.

I Saw an Angel Today

There were many of them arriving at the airport as we
were waiting to board a plane back to Canada.
They had big red crosses on their backs.
They were carrying a lot of equipment and some
were leading search dogs upon their arrival.
We were feeling nervous about being in a foreign country and
started asking people if they knew what was going on.
We were told that there was a massive earthquake and
that help was arriving from all over the World.
We looked at each other in shock and disbelief.
We had been on vacation for a week in that beautiful
tropical island destination and did not feel a thing.
We were on the other side of the Island, snorkeling and
playing with the fish when this huge capital city fell, only
five hundred kilometres away. A **Prince** has fallen.
When we arrived home, we were met by very concerned
family and friends and felt very lucky to be safe.
I have always believed that if people are meant to experience
devastating events such as this, then it does not matter
where they are in the World, they will experience it.
It was an opportunity for us to give Gratitude for our safety,
health, and welfare each and every day that followed.
For months after this event we followed the relief efforts of
the World and witnessed the combined Love of mankind
by thousands. It was inspiring and uplifting.
This event hit very close to our home away from
home and very close to our hearts.
We felt for the families of the lost.
We will never forget them.

I Saw an Angel Today

People were celebrating every-where as he was released
from prison after serving twenty-seven years.
I was wondering why a person who served so much time in
prison had the support of thousands, possibly millions.
He was a South African Apartheid Leader who was
sentenced to life in prison for "sabotage."
There were reports of violence and discourse until
he addressed his followers at City Hall.
I heard that the ANC flag that his supporters flew was
illegal to possess only ten days before his release.
I understood that the leaders of many nations were concerned
about Civil War and lobbied to have him freed.
It was time. It was time to end racial segregation.
It was time to end the violence.
It was time for peace and unity.
I have a strong sense that everything played out perfectly.
I believe he did more good behind bars than he
probably would have done if he was free.
I think that if the prosecution had won, and he was
given the death sentence, he would not have had the
same impact years and even decades later.
I believe in the evolution of man and that things happen
in time. Time that we can all understand.
I think that he understood the essence of time in the end.
On all our paths and our own *Long Walk to Freedom*,
we come to learn and appreciate time.
I am Grateful for the time he spent learning, growing, and
teaching from the parameters of his four walls.
I will never forget him.

I Saw an Angel Today

He has been voted in for a second term. It doesn't surprise me
as he is, in my opinion, one the greatest leaders of all time.
He is doing so many amazing things for the people.
He believes everyone has a right to healthcare.
He is addressing *Climate Change Denial*.
He is not afraid to speak of places like Shishmaref
Alaska being abandoned and disappearing.
He is working on an energy policy for clean energy.
He is brave enough to stand behind gay rights and
legalize marriage for the GLQBT communities.
He even ended a war and brought our soldiers home.
He is the forty-fourth to sit in that famous oval office.
He is the first African American to do the same.
And the first one actually born outside his reign on an Island.
Nine months after Inauguration he was given the 2009 Nobel
Peace Prize Lecture titled "A Just and Lasting Peace."
I wish that he could run for the rest of his life.
I feel so safe and at peace with him at the helm.
I Love watching his Love he expresses for his wife and family.
He is the epitome of all that is good.
I know his job is tough and met with too much criticism
and judgement, but he must be doing something right.
They voted him in again.
I am so relieved.
This is out of our control as we Canadians have no
input, although their homes are right beside ours.
I thank God for his service and his opportunity to keep
doing these amazing things for all people.
I will never forget him.

I Saw an Angel Today

There were countless numbers of them all scrambling
to aid in the largest storm I have ever heard of.
They said that this is just the beginning, but I am hopeful.
She has been named as one of the five deadliest
hurricanes in the history of the country she hit.
She left an aftermath of unbelievable proportion.
She may have caused great destruction, but she has also
created the most amazing positive outcome.
I always wondered what would happen if something
catastrophic were to happen to us humans.
How would we react? Would we band together or separate?
Would we just look out for number one, or everyone?
Would we realize that we are ultimately all the same?
Just humans, having a human experience.
My questions were answered as I watched the pouring
in of assistance from all over the World.
What touched me the most is that even the assumed enemies of
this affected country, offered up more than could be imagined by
anyone knowing the history of the two country's discourse.
Aid from all over the World flooded in.
Even parts of the World perceived as poor or "Third
World Country," offered everything they could.
This is the World I am proud to be living in.
This is the outcome I hoped and prayed for.
This is the kind of kindness that I hoped for my children,
grandchildren, and great-grandchildren.
They will remember her name for years to come.
I hope they remember what she taught us.
I will never forget her.

I Saw an Angel Today

There were hundreds and maybe thousands of our trained,
brave, and strong forces of Defense and Peace.
In the past ten years, they had captured and killed two
of the biggest terrorist leaders of our time.
They risked their lives and sought out justice for
thousands of innocent lives around the World.
I have always been against fighting and killing of our
brothers and sisters on this planet, but times like these make
me feel safe and protected. Grateful for their efforts.
I am still so surprised that the areas that were once considered
the holiest of lands, were now such a threat.
I am hopeful that they will return to the peace we all want.
As the news spread of these captures and subsequent deaths of these two
horrible men, I was Grateful for all the forces that worked hard to find them
and bring them to justice. More than justice served was a feeling of security.
Some say that this will just create more anger and revenge, but
I think they have proven that peace will ultimately win.
I cannot imagine where we might be today, if we did
not come together to seek peace and justice.
I can feel the brotherhood of the nations.
I can feel the relief of the people around the World.
I know that these events of the last ten years have created a bond of nations
and an understanding of force required to achieve a peaceful outcome.
I think about all the lives lost.
I am so Grateful for all the lives saved.
We will never forget them.

I Saw an Angel Today

There was a horrible oil spill that has been named
the fifty-fourth largest spill in history.
What made this one seemingly worse than the previous ranking one's, is the
long-lasting effects it has had on the land and water around it, decades later.
It spilled more than ten million gallons of oil over thirteen hundred
miles of coastline and eleven thousand square miles of ocean.
It killed over two hundred thousand birds including
two hundred and forty-seven eagles.
Over thirty-one hundred seals and otters and
countless salmon and herring were also lost.
It was estimated it would take over thirty years to recover.
I struggled to find a positive outcome to that disaster.
If not for the over eleven thousand humans who spent
countless hours and as much resources to try to gain control
and clean up the area, it would have been much worse.
Over twenty-five years later, sixteen to twenty-one thousand
gallons still remain in the sands and soil of the affected areas.
However, many laws and policies have changed with the introduction
of the common objective of "Safer Ships and Cleaner Oceans."
A new Oil Pollution Act was also implemented, that protects
the areas affected but is also partially responsible for the
new legislation requiring double hulled carriers.
A better result of this crisis would be for humans
to find a better way of fueling our needs.
It will be the Angels on Earth that continue to work
towards these much-needed environment changes.
I will never forget them.

I Saw an Angel Today

It was marked as the hundredth anniversary of the death
of an activist for the Suffragette Movement.
The press reported her actions of that of a madwoman, while
her Suffragette followers hailed her as a martyr.
She attended the greatest British national event as a
spectator and left as one of the most famous women of
the movement that she ultimately gave her life to.
She went to prison nine times and was force fed forty-nine
times, but she was still passionate about women's rights.
At the time is was believed that she tried to commit
suicide as a last attempt of a desperate woman.
As the one hundredth anniversary of her death passes, modern
technology reveals a probable more accurate cause.
It has taken the study of three camera angles to determine
that she appeared to be trying to tie a scarf onto a famous
horse as a publicity stunt. A symbol of her movement.
She knew that all eyes and cameras would be on this famous
horse, and that *The Statement* would be made.
It also appeared that she misjudged the speed and the
horse's reaction as she was bowled over by the horse.
She was taken to a nearby hospital where she slipped
into a comma and died three days later.
She left this planet with a statement that impacted
many, as tens of thousands of people attended her funeral
procession including thousands of Suffragettes.
She definitely earned her wings of change for humanity.
I believe she was one of the bravest women of all time.
I will never forget her.

I Saw an Angel Today

They are now known as the "Los 33."
They were thirty-three miners trapped twenty-three hundred feet
underground and about three miles from the entrance to the mine.
After everything the country had been through with a
recent earthquake followed by a tsunami, the people of that
country had enough empathy to move mountains.
The nations outpouring of concern for the workers and their families led
the National government to take over the search and rescue operation.
That is what probably saved the miners.
As eight exploratory holes were drilled, one drill bit came to the
surface that revealed that all thirty-three miners were fine.
After the world discovered the men were alive,
International efforts were implemented.
After sixty-nine days of being buried alive, all thirty-
three men were rescued with little to no injuries.
During their time underground the men realized that they
would never survive without creating a social system
of their own. A one man one vote democracy.
Their system included a first in command, second
in command, a medic, a religious leader, a pastor, an
energizing comedian, and a communications expert.
That was probably one of the greatest lessons of that horrible
incident. A society that worked together to live peacefully.
As I watched, read, and listened to their stories, I am hopeful
that an accident like this never happens again.
I also feel that there was much more to learn, for *all* of us.
More than just rescue efforts. Maybe a better way of life?
I will never forget them.

I Saw an Angel Today

Billions of Angels around the World are creating fund
raising events and assisting in relief efforts.
There has been a massive earthquake, which created a
devasting tsunami and even a nuclear plant meltdown.
The lives lost, and the damages done are almost too
much for a person like me to comprehend.
I feel so helpless in their hours of need and can only offer
a donation here and there as I see the campaigns.
I believe that every little penny counts in times like these.
People around the World who can barely put food on their
own table, give from their heart and create miracles.
One hundred and sixty-three countries and forty-
eight International organizations offered assistance. Of
those people, are people just like you and me.
Donations totalled over five hundred and twenty billion dollars.
Nine hundred and thirty thousand people have assisted in countless ways.
It amazes me how we come together and offer our time,
extra clothing, furniture, food, money, and energy to our
brothers and sisters on the other side of the planet.
I find it funny that my mind cannot absorb the data of the devastation, but
my heart has no problem with the outpouring of Love offered by all of us.
We are a charitable human race.
When the chips are down we bring the dip.
We are strongest as One.
I am proud of all the charity work I have seen around
the World and in my own back yard.
It doesn't take much to be a Charity Angel.
I will never forget any of them.

I Saw an Angel Today

When I think about Global Events and the effects of the human race, I have
to include the creations of the computers, the internet and social media.
There are hundreds and maybe thousands of Angels responsible
for the information highway that we now have.
It has connected every one of us in countless ways.
It has enhanced and, in some ways, hindered our lives.
Some people speak of the social experiences lost.
Some people are afraid of who might be monitoring us.
Some people choose to keep it as far away as possible.
I think it is like anything in life. We have the tools at hand
and how we choose to use them can have either a negative or
positive affect. I choose to use it in a positive manner.
Searching for things at record speed.
Keeping in touch with family and friends around the World.
Sharing information and messages of hope and Love.
Even the ability to buy something that brings me joy.
Especially music, that I have always considered
the universal language of the World.
It can be created, purchased, shared, and enjoyed.
We can even carry these mini inventions in our hands and
assist each other immediately in countless ways.
Like anything created in the past, from alcohol to hemp, how we choose to
use these things will ultimately create your own experience. Good or Bad.
I am Grateful to every Angel who created the
computers, internet, and social media.
We will never forget them.

What Angels Did you See today?

I Saw an Angel Today

These pages are for you to record names of your own Earth Angels who have impacted your life. Please remember to let them know how they have helped you and how Grateful you are for them.

My Earth Angels

My Earth Angels

About the Author

Marcelline believes that every-one has a story to share from their own life experiences. Through the five major careers she has had, she has gained a variety of her own life experiences to share. While waitressing in small road side restaurants, and working in a men's maximum-security prison, she has met a vast variety of people from which she draws her stories. Marcelline has been on a spiritual path of discovery for most of her life and believes that gratitude is the way to happiness. She has come to experience a gift of seeing everyday people doing amazing things for others, just by staying in gratitude. She shares these stories with her readers.